Sport
and
Fitness

UNCOVERED

CAREERS UNCOVERED

Careers Uncovered guides aim to expose the truth about what it's really like to work in a particular field, containing unusual and thought-provoking facts about the profession you are interested in. Written in a lively and accessible style, *Careers Uncovered* guides explore the highs and lows of the career, along with the job opportunities and skills and qualities you will need to help you make your way forward.

Titles in this series include:

Accountancy Uncovered
Art and Design Uncovered
Charity and Voluntary Work Uncovered
E-commerce Uncovered
Journalism Uncovered
Law Uncovered
Marketing and PR Uncovered
Media Uncovered
Medicine Uncovered
Music Industry Uncovered
Nursing and Midwifery Uncovered
Performing Arts Uncovered
Teaching Uncovered
Travel Industry Uncovered
Working for Yourself Uncovered

trotman

BERYL DIXON

Sport
and
Fitness

UNCOVERED

2ND EDITION

Sport and Fitness Uncovered

This second edition published in 2007 by Trotman
an imprint of Crimson Publishing
Westminster House, Kew Road, Richmond TW9 2ND
www.crimsonpublishing.co.uk

© Trotman 2007

First edition published 2004 by Trotman and Co Ltd
Reprinted 2005

Editorial and Publishing Team

Author Beryl Dixon
Editorial Mina Patria, Publishing Director; Jessica Spencer,
Development Editor; Jo Jacomb, Editorial Manager; Ian Turner,
Production Editor
Production John O'Toole, Operation Manager

Designed by XAB

British Library Cataloguing in Publication Data
A catalogue record for this book is available from the
British Library

ISBN 978 1 84455 121 7

Typeset by Mac Style, East Yorkshire
Printed and bound by Creative Print and Design, Wales

CONTENTS

About the author

Beryl Dixon is an experienced careers adviser who has worked for different local education authorities and in a tertiary college where she helped students of all ages with their decisions on both higher education and employment. She also worked for the Ministry of Defence and the Department for Education and Skills, visiting schools in Brussels, Luxembourg, Cyprus and Hong Kong to provide careers advice to the children of expatriate personnel and government officials.

She now concentrates on careers writing and is the author of several books, including *What Can I Do with an Arts Degree?*, *What Can I Do with a Social Science Degree?*, *How to Choose your Postgraduate Course* (Trotman), *Jobs and Careers after A Level and Other Advanced Qualifications* and *Decisions at 16 Plus* (Lifetime Careers Publishing). She also writes for a number of publications, including *YouCan*, UCAS's magazine for A level students, and *Careerscope*, the magazine of the Independent Schools' Careers Organisation.

INTRODUCTION

Any idea how many events take place at the Olympic Games? At the 2012 games in London there will be 300 events in 28 different sports. Around 10,250 competitors are expected to take part. They will have coaches and networks of support staff to help them attain peak fitness and to improve their skills.

Don't worry: you don't have to be an athlete of such standing to enjoy a career in sport and fitness!

WHY READ THIS BOOK?

Because you have started to think about careers. It's never too early to do so. There are dozens of jobs out there. Some would be right for you; some wouldn't. Some you will be qualified to do; others you won't. That said, you still have a pretty wide choice – and you want to get it right. So by starting here you are beginning your research into which job or jobs are likely to be best for you. You will be able to work out which careers fit best with your:

● interests

● personality

● skills

● values.

WHY THINK OF A CAREER IN SPORT AND FITNESS?

'Because I enjoy it,' you'll probably say. 'And because I can be paid to spend all day doing something I enjoy.' Right. Those are two very good reasons. A third is that these are areas that offer plenty of jobs. Everywhere you look there are gyms, health clubs, recreation and leisure centres – many privately owned, some attached to hotels, some owned by local authorities (although these are usually contracted out to commercial firms to manage). Then there is the fact that you will benefit personally. You will be fit and healthy yourself!

WHY ARE THERE SO MANY JOBS?

- The sport and recreation industries are growing. They now employ over 621,000 people in the UK and the sector continues to create one in four new jobs. (Source: Institute for Sport, Parks and Leisure (ISPAL).)

- People are spending more on leisure activities and fitness. According to the TUC the average working week in Britain is 43.5 hours. Take out time spent in travelling to and from work and in doing household chores and other necessary stuff, and there's quite a lot of time left for leisure. If you opt for a career in sport and fitness you can be involved in your work in something that other people pay to do. But it *will* be work! Don't forget that.

- People of all ages and income levels are able to spend time and/or money on health and fitness. People who have been able to take early retirement take up golf, swimming or rambling, or take out membership of a health club. Some older people who are able to come in at quiet times take up an off-peak membership in a health club, and can take part in classes from a choice of dozens. Unemployed people and students also benefit from concessions at off-peak times. Some high earners, celebrities and stressed professionals see the benefits of staying fit and healthy. People like Madonna and Tony Blair are widely rumoured to employ personal trainers. Some well-off clients have their own home gyms where trainers come to them. Christianne

Wolff (see pages 41–3) has some famous people among her clients.

- Some people enjoy being active. Others are encouraged or bullied into it. They read newspaper articles promoting healthy lifestyles or are advised to take up some form of physical activity by their doctor. (Some doctors recommend swimming or supervised gym workouts to patients with conditions ranging from heart disease to obesity.)

Not too high a risk of unemployment, then. But what about pay? It is not as great as in some industries – but real job satisfaction can go a long way to compensate. You could earn your living doing something you enjoy – an extension of a hobby, in fact (a hopeless dream for many stuck in jobs they dislike) – but you are unlikely to earn a fortune. We can't all be David Beckham or Serena Williams. It is difficult to make a living in professional sport – and only a very few very highly paid individuals make it to the top. Most professional sportsmen/women also have other jobs to support themselves. But there are literally dozens of other jobs in sport and fitness. Some of them pay well; others less so. Employers can sometimes get away with paying less to enthusiasts and rely on job satisfaction being more important to their employees than loads of cash.

This book, like others in the series, will give you the lowdown on these jobs. In the book you will find job descriptions, factual information on training, prospects and likely earnings. You'll also find out about the downsides. This book gives you the truth – warts and all. Throughout the book are case studies. You can read first-hand what people in the sports and fitness industries say for themselves about their work. And you can read their tips and advice.

WHAT DO SOME SPORTS PROFESSIONALS SAY?

Manager of a large local authority leisure centre with over 200 staff

What do you like about your job?
'Dealing with the public. It's never dull.'

And dislike?
'The bureaucracy. I spend ages on form-filling and conducting risk assessments. There is a shedful of legislation on public health and safety. But it is necessary.'

PE teacher in a large comprehensive school

What do you like about your job?
'Being able to indulge my own passion for sport. I teach the full range of team sports and am able to coach one I really love after school. There is a buzz in seeing my team win matches all season.'

And dislike?
'The problem of getting girls motivated. Sport isn't cool and there is a lot of peer pressure to conform and drop out of activities as they get higher up the school.'

Self-employed personal fitness trainer

What do you like about your job?
'The sheer variety. I meet so many different people – and all their programmes are different. Plus I love helping people to achieve.'

And dislike?
'Having to do all my own paperwork and accounts.'

Sports development officer

What do you like about your job?
'I don't like it. I love it.'

And dislike?
'The unsocial hours are a drawback. I don't mind giving up some weekends to attend events or do some coaching but I also have to go to a lot of evening meetings.'

Sports physiotherapist

What do you like about your job?
'The flexibility. I can work the hours I choose. And I get to meet a variety of patients.'

And dislike?
'Not much. But being self-employed I don't take much holiday.'

YOUR TURN

So, how about becoming a personal trainer? Sport development officer? Swimming teacher? Leisure centre manager? Sports psychologist?

Careers covered in this book include those in the main areas of:

- sport

- physical fitness and education

- leisure and recreation

- and other areas such as health and media work.

THE FUTURE

The sector is expected to continue outperforming the UK economy's growth rate until 2014 with output reaching up to £11.9 billion (SkillsActive, February 2007).

CHAPTER 1

The truth about sport and fitness

You probably know something about the most popular sports and activities – especially if you practise one of them. But did you know that the following all have official websites?

● Beach volleyball

● curling

● freestyle skiing

● luge.

Look on Yahoo's sports directory webpages for more information (http://dir.yahoo.com/Recreation/Sports/).

WHY SHOULD YOU THINK ABOUT A CAREER IN SPORT AND FITNESS?

According to the Institute for Sports, Parks and Leisure (ISPAL) the leisure industry is huge, with a wide range of job opportunities. Because it's a relatively new and expanding industry there are many opportunities for gaining qualifications and finding employment. In some jobs it is possible to progress by gaining experience and obtaining qualifications while working (for example NVQ/SVQs). In more senior posts it is more usual to have formal qualifications in addition to experience.

- (With variations across the industry) there are lots of jobs that do not require too many paper qualifications.

- There are also increasing openings for people with degrees.

- Many careers are genuinely open in terms of opportunities. Once you've found the first job, promotion to all levels is possible.

Advancement in some careers, however, does require qualifications in addition to experience.

You could start from various entry points:

- from school at 16/17 years old with some exam passes – or with no formal qualifications

- from school/college at 18/19 years old with A levels or Scottish Highers

- from school/college at 18/19 years old with a vocational qualification

- from higher education with an HND, a foundation degree or honours degree

- from higher education with a postgraduate qualification

- from another career with relevant experience.

And according to Sports Coach UK (the national coaching federation), the Government Agenda for Sport means that there will be:

- a massive increase in after-school sport and inter-school competition

- a rapid rise in young people (under 19 years old) involved in sports leadership and volunteering, linked to the inclusion of citizenship on the national curriculum

- an increase in sports programmes designed to tackle wider social issues (law and order, health, and social exclusion.)

Which means – more jobs!

DEFINITIONS FIRST

What is the difference between sport and fitness; and what is 'leisure', for that matter?

Sport and fitness are part of the wider leisure and hospitality industry – which is enormous. It already employs more than 2.5 million people in the UK, and is growing. But that figure refers to the whole sector, which includes travel and tourism as well as sport. Some tourism does include sport. There has been a growth in the number and type of adventure holidays that people can take – ranging from white water rafting to trekking. Are these leisure or tourism? No matter: they need qualified instructors. More jobs for people who want to qualify in outdoor pursuits!

So excluding straight holiday tourism, sport and fitness include all sorts of team and individual activities: from badminton to martial arts; cricket to rowing; tennis to fishing; keep fit to circuit training. Not all offer paid employment, however. You have to make the distinction between amateur and professional sport. You can't officially earn a living through athletics, for instance –

except, perhaps, by coaching. But having said that, many amateurs make a decent living from sponsoring products and giving after-dinner speeches ...

SPORT

The main jobs in sport, in which you could be active and play your sport/s, are:

- professional player

- coach

- instructor/teacher.

Then there are openings for people who make sports activities possible. For example:

- leisure centre assistant

- leisure centre manager

- lifeguard/pool attendant

- sports development officer.

And jobs on the sidelines. Sport is not the main skill here. For example:

- administrative, reception and sales staff in recreation and leisure centres

- sports psychologist

- physiotherapist

- sports journalist.

FASCINATING FACT

Did you know that there are 28 sports in the summer Olympics? Do you know what they are? (Answer at end of this chapter.)

And did you know that to be included in the Olympics a sport must be 'widely practised by men in at least 75 countries and on four continents, and by women in at least 40 countries and on three continents'?

FITNESS

Fitness is individual and personal. People have their own priorities and want workouts and routines to help them to achieve them. Jobs in the fitness industry include:

● aerobics teacher

● exercise instructor

● fitness centre/health club manager

● fitness centre/health club assistant

● personal trainer.

These jobs and many others are described in the following chapters. You will also find information on training courses. Training and qualifications are something that you will need to check out very carefully, particularly in the fitness area, where there are some rogue ones about.

WHICH WORKING ENVIRONMENT WOULD SUIT YOU?

Would you like to work?

● In a small team

● with colleagues who come and go on different shifts

- one-to-one with clients

- in a large centre

- in one place

- in different places

- on a cruise ship

- indoors

- outdoors.

Well, you're in luck. In sport and fitness you could work in any of these settings and with any combination of people. On the whole, you are not likely to work in very large organisations, other than the very big city leisure centres, which employ as many as 200 staff. But you could work in any of the following places:

- clients' homes

- colleges

- the countryside

- fitness centres, gyms and health clubs

- hospitals

- leisure and recreation centres

- newspaper offices

- outdoor pursuits centres

- schools

- sports centres

- sports equipment shops

● sports fields

● stadiums

● swimming pools

● TV studios

● your own home.

And in any of the following environments:

● on golf courses

● on grass

● on horseback

● on ice

● on rivers

● in, on or under the sea

● on tracks

● underground.

HOW MUCH COULD YOU REALISTICALLY EXPECT TO EARN?

This is a notoriously difficult sector when it comes to assessing average earnings. Pay rates vary according to size of employer and location. (Pay is usually higher in London and the South East.) Overtime and unsocial hours' allowances could boost your earnings considerably. Many people working in fitness put in what many of us might regard as excessively long hours in overtime (but so does a City banker), and therefore earn much more than any average figures quoted. They would say that they do not regard taking evening keep fit, dance, aerobics or circuit training sessions as work. They enjoy doing it. What do you think?

As a rough guide, however:

Leisure centre assistants may be paid either on an hourly rate or receive an annual salary. Whichever way it is calculated, they are likely to earn from £10,000 to £14,500 per year. This is the basic salary for a working week of about 37 hours. **Leisure centre managers** would earn somewhere between £22,000 and £25,000 per year. Managers of the largest centres earn more – in the region of £40,000 plus a company car.

Many centre assistants and supervisors or junior managers increase their earnings by working evening and weekend shifts for additional payment and by taking classes at the centre in activities for which they are qualified to teach.

Sports coaches – there are very few full-time paid positions. Most of those enthusiastic souls who give up their time to coach pupils after school or junior teams on Saturdays are volunteers doing it for sheer pleasure. Some coaches do work professionally (often combining this work with another job) and can expect to earn from £6 to £20 per hour. Salaries vary according to which sports are coached and at what level. At the very top of the profession some salaries of £60,000 are on offer – and the real top-drawer coaches earn more. A few hold salaried positions with local authorities and can expect to earn £20,000 to £25,000.

Personal trainers are either paid as leisure centre assistants or supervisors, or are self employed. If you look at the website of the National Register of Personal Trainers (www.nrpt.co.uk) you will see adverts from trainers, quoting their range of expertise and their fee levels. Most charge £25 to £30 per hour. In the centre of well-heeled areas – Knightsbridge and Chelsea in London, and some parts of large cities like Leeds and Manchester – some charge over £60. Out of this they have to meet their costs (and time) travelling to visit clients and perhaps fees for booking space and equipment in a gym.

Professional players – the sky's the limit. Or it is for the successful and famous. The B list have to support themselves through other jobs.

Jockeys may be employed on a salaried basis or as freelance. A successful employed jockey could earn over £50,000 – but many earn more by taking a percentage of the prize money.

Pay for **full-time lifeguards** starts at around £10,500 per year. With experience, they can earn £15,000 or more.

Riding instructors don't do very well in the pay stakes since a qualified instructor's starting pay could be £12,000. It could rise to around £18,000, however, and those with the highest qualifications, which means passing lots of exams and becoming a Fellow of the British Horse Society, can demand up to £35,000. An equestrian centre manager could earn £18,000 to £27,000. Needless to say, many of them wouldn't consider doing anything else. Once again, money isn't everything.

Teachers in state schools are paid on salary scales ranging from £20,133 (£24,168 in inner London) to £26,460 (more in inner London). That's if they do not get promoted. If they take on more responsibilities they can earn up to £41,004 in inner London and £34,281 outside London. Heads of large schools can get up to £104,268 (excluding inner London allowance). But then, they are not teaching sport!

PAY AND JOB SATISFACTION IN THE FITNESS INDUSTRY

The organisations SkillsActive and the Register of Exercise Professionals conducted a survey in 2006, which found the average salaries by occupation were:

Director	£33,301
Group/area/regional manager	£31,964
General manager	£27,598
Assistant club manager	£18,508
Club/duty manager	£17,823
Studio or fitness manager	£17,332
Fitness instructor/personal trainer	£16,649
Yoga or Pilates instructor	£14,273
Advanced instructor	£13,915
Exercise to music instructor	£12,295
Gym instructor, Level 2	£12,111

The survey also found that:

- nine in ten people planned to stay in the industry for the next three years

- seven out of ten people would recommend their employers to a friend

- some employees receive an annual bonus – on average 2% of basic salary

- 59% of respondents gave low pay as a factor that might make them consider leaving the fitness industry

- only 2% of directors were dissatisfied with their remuneration packages (message – stick it out and gain promotion?).

Overall, most employees reported a high level of job satisfaction, being pleased with their employers, hours of work and degrees of responsibility.

SOME GENUINE JOB ADVERTS
(These all appeared in leisure and sport magazines or on websites in the spring of 2007.)

Assistant leisure club manager	Jersey	£17–£17.5k
Centre managers (2 posts)	Durham	£20,895–£24,708. Essential car user allowance
Community sports development officer	Surrey	£21,180–£24,912
Community tennis coaches	London	£8,947–£9,463
Fitness/studio manager	Birmingham	£15–£16k
Golf membership sales executive	Staffordshire	£13–15k. OTE £18k
Lecturer in sport and fitness	Milton Keynes	£32,795–£39,160

Leisure assistant	Cumbria	£12,000 + excellent benefits + living-in
Full-time leisure assistant	Central London	£12,000 depending on qualifications
Multi-skill community sports coaches	Dorset	£20,234–£23,457 (pro rata)
Netball development officer	Lancashire	£16,137–£17,985
Senior assistant manager – centre	Lee Valley	£20,100–£23,943
Senior leisure assistant	Suffolk	£14,787 rising to £17,985
Senior leisure development officer (water sports)	London Borough of Merton	£27,084–£28,578
Senior recreation assistants	Northants	£12–14k
Sports and strategy manager	Southampton	£34,146–£42,402
Sports development officer	Leicestershire	£18k
Sports development officer	Hampshire	Starting at £21,946
Swimming development officer	Hampshire	Starting at £21,946

You will notice that the higher up the ladder you go, the fewer actual sports activities your job will involve. But this is the pattern in most jobs. Chief constables don't patrol the streets; head teachers don't work in the classroom; hotel managers don't wait in restaurants ...

IS SPORT AND FITNESS FOR YOU?

SPORTS QUIZ

1. You have just finished a hard day's teaching in a secondary school. You have a pile of GCSE PE coursework to mark. You want to go home, have something to eat and then get on with them. A 14-year-old pupil comes along and asks whether you could spare 15 minutes to come and encourage the football team by discussing tactics with them.

Do you:

a) Say you've got too many other things to do?
b) Arrange another time?
c) Put your car keys away and go to the pitch?

2. You are a sports development officer at a meeting of city councillors. You're trying to raise funds to develop coaching in a poor area of the city to keep the kids off the street. One councillor is particularly obstructive – he thinks they should make their own entertainment.

Do you:

a) Tell him he's a dinosaur? Kids may have played quietly and stayed in during the war but this is 2007.
b) Explain carefully that this a way of discouraging youth crime and making the area safer for the community?
c) Sigh and look to heaven for support?

3. You coach a hockey team on Saturdays. Other things – holidays, invitations – keep cropping up and you can't always be there.

Do you:

a) Cancel the sessions? After all, you are giving your time free of charge.
b) Resign and hand over to someone else?
c) Make a list of which invitations are most important and find another coach to cover for you on a small number of occasions?

4. You are a leisure centre manager. You have a friend who is a journalist.

Do you:

a) Constantly feed him with stories, hoping to get the leisure centre mentioned in the paper?
b) Decide that using friends like that is wrong?
c) Get your photograph in his paper as often as you can?

5. You work as a leisure centre assistant. You supervisor suggests that you attend evening classes to gain further qualifications. You can re-organise your shifts in order to go.

Do you:

a) Say 'She must be joking. Do this in my own time?'
b) Accept gratefully?
c) Ask for help with paying the fees?

Answers

1. b) is probably the right answer – because you are genuinely busy; but if you can manage to re-jig your commitments, c) – going to help them now – would be brilliant. Answer a)? You shouldn't be considering this work if you are not prepared to give up time to encourage young players.
2. b) is correct. You will need tact and diplomacy in this line of work. Sometimes it's necessary to be very patient and make other people see your point of view. Did you answer a)? You do want the funding, don't you?
3. c) is correct. You can't be expected to give up everything. But what happened to commitment? Most jobs in sport involve unsocial hours – and you knew this when you took on the job.
4. a) is good – but why not tone it down a little? Send him a list of possible stories and offer to discuss them with him. Answer c)? Whatever happened to teamwork? Don't other members of staff deserve their 15 minutes of fame too?
5. Answer c) is OK. You are showing that you are keen to get on, but as you don't earn very much it's fair to make the request. Did you answer a)? What a way to show commitment! You do want to progress, don't you?

FITNESS QUIZ

1. You're a fitness instructor and have had a really hard day at the gym. Clients were grumpy and wouldn't co-operate.

Do you:

a) Go home in tears?
b) Shrug it off? You can't win 'em all. Tomorrow will be better.
c) Think about a nice job in an office?

2. You are a personal trainer. A client simply isn't putting in the effort.

Do you:

a) Think 'Oh, well. His loss. He's paying me, after all'?
b) Nag and bully until he gives it a bit more welly?
c) Spend some time working out a different programme?

3. You have raised the finance and managed to open your own fitness centre. Money's tight, though.

Do you:

a) Hire staff who seem competent? You can watch them at work and see how well they perform.
b) Make sure that they have approved qualifications?
c) Recruit people who already do sessions in other clubs? They must be OK if they're working there.

4. You need to bring in clients to your club.

Do you:

a) Pay for newspaper advertising?
b) Print leaflets and have them put through letter boxes?
c) Get friends to spread the word?

5. You are a gym manager. Prospective clients ask to be shown around.

Do you:

a) Do it yourself?
b) Do the tour and take a junior member of staff with you to observe?
c) Delegate it to your deputy?

Answers
1. b) is correct. You have to take the rough with the smooth. In any job that involves work with people – not just in this industry – there are bound to be days when you have personality clashes or problems of some kind. Answer a) or c)? Are you a wimp or what?
2. c) is the right answer. Personal trainers need to motivate their clients and make the sessions enjoyable. You do this by thinking that maybe your programme needs modifying, not by barking like a sergeant major.
3. Don't even think about a) or c). What would happen if there were some kind of accident or a client made a claim for negligence or incorrect teaching? You will need comprehensive insurance – and you won't get it if you employ unqualified staff. It's up to you to check this and not to assume that another employer has been conscientious.
4. b) and/or c). Answer a) is OK – but pricey.
5. Any answer is correct (assuming that your deputy is competent!). Training someone else to do the job – b) – would be a good move though.

IS THE JOB RIGHT FOR YOU?

CORE SKILLS IN SPORT
The core skills that every sportsperson needs – whether player, teacher or coach – are:

● a positive attitude

● ability in one or more sports

- ability to motivate others

- communication skills

- enthusiasm

- generosity (to others on the pitch)

- leadership

- organisational skills

- patience

- self-discipline

- some knowledge of psychology

- stamina

- teamwork skills

- willingness to work unsocial hours.

'If you are interested in becoming a leisure assistant it is essential that you are self-confident and not shy talking to people. You have to be able to make yourself heard and be assertive – particularly if you are managing a situation that could be a potential hazard to the public (e.g. if someone gets into difficulty in the pool). Being able to make quick decisions and to take control of the situation is vital.'

Adam Dodd, Leisure Assistant

'Without a doubt communication skills are essential in this job. You need to be a people person as you are dealing with members of the public all day. You also need to be prepared to work long hours.'

Garry Peal, Leisure Centre Manager

CORE SKILLS IN FITNESS

The core skills needed are:

- a positive attitude

- ability in one or more activities

- ability to motivate others

- ability to be firm when necessary

- communication

- diplomacy

- enthusiasm

- knowledge of health and safety

- knowledge of physiology and anatomy

- leadership

- organisational skills

- patience

- perseverance

- self-discipline

- some knowledge of psychology

- willingness to work unsocial hours.

Skills you need in this job include organisational ability – there are a lot of different areas of work; communication skills – it is vital to keep members happy; and leadership. You have to act as a role model for staff.'

Sue Hornibrook, Assistant Health Club Manager

The most important skills for a personal trainer are patience and communication skills. You have to be able to react to each client as an individual. Sometimes it's necessary to be assertive. At other times you have to coax. It also helps to be creative. I get bored easily myself, which helps me to see when clients are becoming bored with their programme. I then adapt it and try different activities.'

Christianne Wolff, Personal Trainer

WHAT WILL THE HOURS BE LIKE?

One – variable. Two – unsocial. (Luckily for them few people working in sport and leisure have working hours as unsocial as those of Chris Hollins, who presents sports reports on BBC's *Breakfast* at 6.10am, 7.32am and 8.32am every weekday. On the BBC website he says that the most difficult thing is going to bed. 'My body wants to go to sleep at seven-ish but my mind wants to stay up and watch TV until late. Waking up in the dark isn't much fun. It's going to be a constant battle. Rob Bonnet (his predecessor, who used to get up at 3.45am) did warn me!')

You will have to work when other people are free. You can say goodbye to having every weekend free. And you will have to work some evenings. In many jobs you will work on a shift or rota system. This can play havoc with your own social life – but a good manager or supervisor should work out duty rotas well in advance so that staff know what shifts they have been assigned, and can change them with colleagues if necessary.

This is not so very different from the conditions experienced by nurses; doctors; other people employed in the health service, such as paramedics and porters; people who work in hotels; police officers; firefighters; and many more – shop assistants too, now that some stores open seven days a week, and sometimes 24 hours a day.

HOW IMPORTANT TO YOU IS MONEY?
Have you picked up the point about not earning megabucks in this industry? (It's been mentioned ...)

FREELANCE WORK
Do you dream of being your own boss? Many people do. Some thrive; others can't hack it.

The sport and fitness industry is full of freelance (or self-employed) people. Many of them combine several jobs in order to earn a living – working sessions here and there. Some people just want to be in sole charge of their work; and they work freelance even though they could work for an employer.

Freelance opportunities in sport and fitness include working as:

- aerobics instructors

- coaches

- dance teachers

- keep fit instructors

- personal trainers

- physiotherapists – many combine private sports-injury work with NHS work

- players in some non-team sports – e.g. tennis, golf

- sports journalists

- sports photographers

- sports psychologists

- swimming teachers

- yoga teachers.

If you do go down the freelance route you have to be confident that you can earn enough money, bring in enough work, manage your time, buy any equipment you need, handle your own tax and insurance payments – and do all your own administration.

There are rewards:

- you're independent

- you can choose your own hours of work

- you can decide when to go on holiday

- you can work just as hard as you choose to.

And there are downsides:

- you'll have no job security

- you'll have to think ahead all the time about getting more work

- you'll have to make arrangements for both professional indemnity and heath insurance. (Who pays the bills if you're off sick?)

'When I was building up my private practice, if a client wanted an appointment at three o'clock on a Saturday afternoon – they got one!'
Gill Driver, Physiotherapist

For anyone working in this area the hours vary and most instructors find that they have to work long hours in the summer. My work as a freelance certainly keeps me very busy between March and

October, when I frequently have to turn down offers of work, then drops between autumn and spring. I do try to keep weekends free – and usually manage to do so, which is not usual for most outdoor pursuits instructors. Demand for tuition is normally highest then.'

Claudia Sarner, Outdoor Pursuits Instructor

'I have to be very organised. I have to work when clients want me – which means a lot of early morning and evening work. To compensate, I no longer work at the weekend. I have to plan my work carefully and try to make appointments for clients at the gym one after another. I also arrange home visits for clients who live near to each other on the same day in order to avoid too much driving between appointments. If this is not possible I might add a charge for travelling time to my fee. It necessary to set my own fees and do my accounts. have to be careful not to fill the whole week with bookings. Some time has to be set aside for promoting the business and getting future work.'

Christianne Wolff, Personal Trainer

Even Christianne, who is very successful, says that there are periods when she does not earn very much – or is waiting for payment from clients to come through.

FASCINATING FACTS: ANSWER

The sports included in the summer Olympics are:

- Aquatics (diving, swimming, synchronised swimming and water polo)

- Archery

- Athletics (track and field)

- Badminton

- Baseball

- Basketball

- Boxing

- Canoe/kayak (kayak flatwater and canoe/kayak slalom)

- Cycling (road cycling, track cycling, mountain bike and BMX racing)

- Equestrianism

- Fencing

- Football

- Gymnastics (artistic gymnastics, rhythmic gymnastics and trampolining)

- Handball

- Hockey

- Judo

- Modern pentathlon

- Rowing

- Sailing

- Shooting

- Softball

- Table tennis

- Tae kwon do

- Tennis

- Triathlon

- Volleyball

- Weightlifting

- Wrestling

Of course, there are many more individual sports (300, as we saw in the Introduction): these are broad categories. Aquatics, for instance, includes four disciplines: swimming, diving, water polo and synchronised swimming. Cycling includes road cycling, track cycling, mountain bike and BMX racing. Athletics covers a number of activities in track and field.

CHAPTER 2

What could you be in sport and fitness?

Sports:
Athletics, badminton, ballooning, basketball, bobsleigh, bowling, boxing, canoeing, caving, climbing, cricket, cycling, diving, fencing, figure skating, football, gliding, golf, gymnastics, hang gliding, hockey, ice dance, judo, karate, lacrosse, motor racing, netball, orienteering, parachuting, riding, rowing, rugby, sailing, scuba diving, shooting, show jumping, snooker, squash, table tennis, tae kwon do, tennis, volleyball, water skiing, wind surfing, wrestling.

Fitness:
Aerobics, aqua classes, body conditioning, boxercise, circuit training, dance, fit ball, Pilates, spinning, t'ai chi, tap, weights, yoga.

You can't make a fortune in all of these. Many are amateur sports. But they all offer some earning opportunities – as coaches and instructors if not as professionals.

JOBS IN SPORT AND FITNESS

COACH
Sports coaches train, advise and motivate athletes and sportsmen/women, whether amateur or professional. They provide

feedback on performance, sometimes using videos to help demonstrate weaknesses, and to analyse potential for improvement. If working with professionals, they have to make sure that the sportsperson is able to cope mentally before each big event. Opportunities vary from sport to sport. Professional sports such as football and cricket have traditionally had full-time coaches, but other sports, including horse riding, golf and tennis, also use coaches. Full-time positions for coaching professionals are scarce. There are over 500,000 coaches/instructors in the UK. Only 20% of these are paid; the other 80% are volunteers. Some coach part time, and many are self-employed and work for several clubs or teams.

FITNESS INSTRUCTOR

People who take exercise or fitness classes are usually known as instructors, as opposed to personal trainers who work with individual clients. Exercise and fitness instructors might specialise in one or more – often two or three – of the following: aerobics, aqua exercise, circuit training, keep fit, resistance training, step, weight training and yoga. They must be able to carry out fitness assessments and advise clients on activities that they can undertake safely.

- The majority of employers (72%) in exercise and fitness are small organisations with fewer than ten employees.

- Very few organisations employ more than 25 people.

- More women than men work in exercise and fitness.

Information from SkillsActive.

GROUNDSMAN

Players expect a perfectly kept pitch or course. Groundsmanship is a highly skilled job. Groundsmen maintain pitches for several sports – bowls, cricket, football, rugby, tennis and so on. Their duties include tractor- and hand-mowing, marking out and repairing pitches and keeping them in tip-top condition for matches. Greenkeepers are specialists employed by golf clubs. (See John Ledgwidge's story, page 65.)

HEALTH CLUB MANAGER AND ASSISTANT MANAGER

This job can vary considerably in different clubs. Some managers do some fitness training themselves while others concentrate on managing and developing the business. They are responsible for recruiting and training staff; organising staff rotas; making sure that the club meets health and safety requirements and procedures; managing a budget for staff salaries, purchase and maintenance of equipment; plus advertising and marketing. They also find out exactly what their customers want by talking to them or devising questionnaires, then make sure that these activities are offered. They also deal with any requests and complaints. They are usually on a profit-related salary with targets to achieve.

JOCKEY

Careers begin either as apprentice jockeys (flat racing) or conditional jockeys (jump racing). They are required to undergo short training courses at one of two approved centres in the UK (Newmarket and Doncaster). If they successfully complete the training they are usually offered apprenticeships by trainers who recruit from the schools. At the end of the apprenticeship the trainer applies for a licence for them to ride in races.

Jockeys become professionals in flat racing at the age of 25, or after riding 95 winners. In jump racing they become professionals at the age of 26, or after riding 65 winners. Jockeys must possess a licence from the Jockey Club to be allowed to ride in public races.

Most jockeys are retired by the age of 40. A few become assistant trainers and trainers.

LEISURE (OR RECREATION) ASSISTANT

This job is at the front end, keeping the centre going. Be prepared for hard work – some of it boring, like cleaning changing rooms, moving and repairing equipment, and getting areas of the centre ready for different activities. It's all essential work – and you are highly unlikely to get a job higher up the ladder until you have experience at this level. The job – which involves meeting clients and has variety – can be satisfying in itself. However, promotion prospects are good if you're prepared to work hard and take additional qualifications.

Leisure assistants might sometimes help out at reception, answering the telephone, taking bookings and hiring out equipment such as rackets. They might also take turns working in the cafes and bars, serving food and drinks and running children's birthday parties – organising games or swimming and supervising tea.

ADAM DODD – LEISURE ASSISTANT

Adam is a leisure assistant at Cocks Moors Woods Sports and Leisure Centre in Birmingham. His responsibilities include working as a lifeguard, setting up the sports hall, looking after equipment, being responsible for the general cleanliness of the centre and looking after the public who use the leisure centre.

He keeps up to date with regular training. Staff receive two hours' training every fortnight, and an update of his National Pool Lifeguard Qualification every two months ensures that Adam always has the most recent knowledge in this field. Other training he has undertaken includes first aid at work, health and safety, spinal injuries, lifting and handling, complaints handling and customer care.

He has recently been selected for training as a future manager. His next career move would be to gain promotion to senior leisure assistant, then assistant manager and eventually centre manager. He is doing as much personal development and getting as many qualifications as he can in order to achieve this goal.

On a typical day Adam starts by checking all the areas that the public will be using, making sure the alarms are working and the changing areas are clean and safe etc. He will then be on duty, walking around the centre, monitoring the activities that are going on and checking that everything is running smoothly. Adam also has poolside duty every day. There are normally four leisure assistants on duty at the pool at any time, and they are not only responsible for the safety of the bathers and spectators, but also check that each other is OK. If one of them has to perform a rescue they will need the support of the rest of the team to manage the situation.

The enjoyable side
One of the aspects of his job that Adam enjoys most is meeting people and dealing with the public. 'You need to like talking to people or this job would be very difficult as it is very rare to have a day when you don't need to advise someone or maybe deal with a complaint.' There is a good atmosphere where he works and this is one of the reasons that he really enjoys his job. He works in a supportive team and says they do activities both in and out of work that help build up trust and co-operation between them. 'When you are dealing with the safety of the public and handling emergency situations, you need to be able to trust your colleagues and know what they are capable of.'

And the downsides
One of the things that Adam doesn't like so much is the rota system. 'Working shifts makes it hard to plan things, but you do get used to it quite quickly.' He works 36.5 hours per week on a three-week shift rotation. He works set shifts every Monday, Tuesday and Thursday; then, depending on what week it is, he could be on a late shift on Friday night and early on Saturday and Sunday, or vice versa. He gets every third weekend off.

Adam's advice
'You should get as many qualifications as possible if you want to move up the career ladder. It is also useful to get yourself into a leisure environment as soon as possible – maybe getting a part-time job while you are studying. Academic qualifications are really important, but you also need to learn how to deal with the public, and you can learn a lot from other more experienced people.'

LEISURE CENTRE MANAGER

This job is likely to be based in a much larger centre where there will be a general manager and several assistant managers, each taking charge of some aspects of running the centre. A large leisure centre might hold children's parties, rent rooms for receptions, conferences and exhibitions and have a number of coffee shops and restaurants, and a beauty salon, in addition to sports courts and fitness suites.

NEIL THOMAS – MANAGER, MACCLESFIELD LEISURE CENTRE
Neil is the manager of a large local authority-run leisure centre which has approximately 500,000 people attendances (i.e. not that number of individual clients) each year, and 100 staff. His is a wide-ranging role with many different responsibilities including customer care, finance, health and safety, marketing, human resources etc.

'In fact,' he says, 'if you look at my job description, it's frightening!'

The centre, which is owned by Macclesfield Borough Council, has a multi-purpose sports hall that can be set up to accommodate many sports, including badminton, short tennis, bowls and boccia and a number of different team sports like basketball, football and netball. The sports hall can also be used for children's parties and special events such as exhibitions and schools' music festivals and has been used by the Royal Shakespeare Company and the Hallé orchestra in the past.

The swimming pools include a 25m competition-standard pool, teaching and toddlers' pools. Other facilities include a climbing wall, soft play area, fitness zone (gym), aerobics studio, activity suite and a national-standard athletics track with clubhouse and solarium. There is also a café and a bar, which are contracted out on a concession basis.

Neil has a varied workforce to manage, including two full-time duty managers and two part-time managers, senior recreation assistants who act as junior managers, recreation assistants, whose main role is to work as lifeguards poolside, two back office staff, eight part-time receptionists, and a number of coaches and instructors who run various activity sessions – not to mention the bank of staff who cover sessions, classes or shifts on a casual basis. The cleaners are contracted in and supplied by a specialist cleaning company. 'As you might guess, there is a lot of human resources work in my role – from recruitment and selection to handling conduct and conflict issues.'

Neil's role, although based on normal office hours, requires long hours of work and flexibility in meeting operational and customer needs. As manager, he works mainly from Monday to Friday but also during evenings and weekends when necessary.

What does he do during a typical day? 'First of all there is no such thing! I can come in with the best of intentions to catch up with all the paperwork and then something happens to take me away from it. I do a huge amount of firefighting – in other words dealing with situations as they arise. I try to start the day with a building check and to pick up on operational, health and safety, and customer care issues. However, I could spend as much as 25% of my working day at my computer, answering emails and planning or dealing with various issues.

'Even as centre manager I find myself helping out with operational tasks, e.g. helping with sports hall changeovers of equipment, or on the reception front desk at busy times. There is and has to be a team culture among all the staff for the centre to run smoothly.

'I am expected to attend many meetings, some of which take me away from the centre, and which probably account for at least 10% of my time. I try to ensure that I continue to spend as much time as possible in "managing by walking about," being seen by staff and customers, seeing the issues for myself and trying to be an approachable presence. I really enjoy meeting the customers. That is one of the huge benefits of the job. Customers are usually in a good frame of mind. They are here because they want to be and are hopefully enjoying themselves.

'We can make a big difference to people's lives, teaching them life skills such as how to swim, nursing them back to fitness after illness or injury and generally improving their health and wellbeing. It can be a very rewarding job.'

Is there anything Neil dislikes about his job? 'It's natural to always want to offer more and to be able to improve services and facilities more quickly. However, resources are limited and so as a manager you have to make the tough decisions that are not always popular. I always have to make the best use of what I have at my disposal.'

Neil's background
'I came into this career later than some people do so I had several different jobs before I decided that this was what I wanted to do. I have been a firefighter, forklift truck operator and a chemical process operator, among other occupations – all of which taught me skills that are useful in this career. There is no doubt that good communication skills and a sense of humour have come in handy and a flexible approach to work–life balance is crucial. When I decided to move into the leisure industry I started as a lifeguard after gaining my NPLQ qualification. Next I became a fitness instructor, and then I gained promotion to manager of a health and fitness suite. My next step was to duty manager and then I became the site manager of a smaller leisure centre in the borough.'

Neil has reached his present position by taking charge of his own career development. He has taken advantage of all the internal training offered and has also attended courses in his own time and sometimes at his own expense. He has also done some distance learning study in order to obtain the ISRM Management Certificate.

Neil's advice
'If you begin at the bottom it is perfectly possible to work your way up to a management position. But you must be prepared to work hard and be proactive in your development. Never miss any opportunity to attend any courses your employer offers. Importantly – be prepared to volunteer to take on extra responsibilities and always be ready to cover the next job up if someone is away as you will get yourself noticed and managers will remember you and how useful you hopefully were to the organisation!'

LIFEGUARD/POOL ATTENDANT

Pool attendants patrol the side of the pool (or sit in the chair), looking out for swimmers who seem hesitant or likely to go out of their depth and watching to make sure that no one runs along the side of the pool or jumps into the water in a dangerous way. If anyone is in danger in the water, the pool attendant first throws them a rope or flotation aid and helps them to the edge. If necessary, one attendant dives in to perform a rescue while another asks all other swimmers to leave the pool. They may have to perform resuscitation at the side of the pool. To work as a pool lifeguard you have to be at least 16 years old and must have one of the following qualifications.

- The National Pool Lifeguard Qualification, awarded by the Royal Life Saving Society UK. (Courses are run at local pools and approved training centres. Contact the RLSS for full details.)

- The Swimming Teachers' Association (STA) Level 2 Certificate National Rescue Standard Pool Lifeguard (NaRSPL).

Pool attendants might be responsible for pool maintenance, which involves checking levels of chemicals and water temperature. In some leisure centres they may also work as general leisure assistants and have a mix of pool and dryside duties.

- The Royal Lifesaving Society has over 75,000 lifeguards on its database and trains over 30,000 pool and beach lifeguards each year.

- Lifeguards are employed by local councils, leisure centres, private clubs, schools, colleges, hotels and holiday centres. Beach lifeguards work on beaches across the UK and are employed by local authorities or private companies.

- With further training, lifeguards may advance to supervisory and management roles.

OUTDOOR PURSUITS INSTRUCTOR

There are 900 licensed providers of outdoor activities in the UK. This is a growing industry, although there is still strong competition for jobs.

There are opportunities in activity centres run by private firms, local authorities and charities, leisure centres with climbing walls, and with expedition companies that organise overseas trips.

Instructors usually specialise in one or more activities – such as mountaineering, rock climbing, orienteering, riding or water sports such as sailing, canoeing and wind surfing – and teach them to small groups of people. They need professional qualifications such as those from the British Canoe Union, Mountain Leaders Training UK or a Walking Group Leader Award. All instructors need a first aid certificate, and those teaching water sports also need a lifesaving qualification.

- There are around 78,000 outdoor pursuits instructors, who can find opportunities throughout the country. However, there is severe competition for posts.

- Many instructors are freelance, either working for centres on contract, or directly with clients.

- There are almost as many seasonal and casual jobs as permanent posts in outdoor activities.

- More men than women work in outdoor activities.

In November 2006 the Schools' Minister Jim Knight, launching the *Manifesto for Learning Outside the Classroom*, said that the government was keen to see more children participating in outdoor activities and estimated that many pupils were missing

out on these activities because of teachers' and parents' fears of
accidents. In fact, there had been just seven fatal accidents since
1993. He said that OFSTED would have a clear role in ensuring
that local authorities 'monitor consistently and effectively the safe
management of activities' and that 'a package of guidance will be
developed which will emphasise the need for high-quality
experiences, hopefully putting to an end some of the more
dubious visits organised by some schools.' Perhaps this means
that there will be more opportunities for properly qualified
instructors.

CLAUDIA SARNER – OUTDOOR PURSUITS INSTRUCTOR
Claudia did not take a typical route to qualifying as an
outdoor pursuits instructor. Nor, she says, has she followed
a particularly standard career path. What she has achieved
is a personally satisfying career that contains a lot of variety.

She left school with A levels in Biology, Chemistry and
Physics and an AS in Maths, and went to Leicester University
to do a BSc in Combined Science (mainly Geology and
Biology) 'with no idea at all about a future career. I studied
those subjects for sheer enjoyment. My career decision was
made really on the basis of activities that I was already
doing in my spare time. I had been a scout leader for years
and I did a lot of outdoor activities in my spare time.

'One of my summer jobs had been as an instructor at
Leicester Outdoor Pursuits Centre, a registered charity
which provides high-quality services. They are superb at
paddle sports and are highly regarded by the British Canoe
Union. They also offer climbing, quad biking, ropes courses,
team games, orienteering, archery, fencing and rifle
shooting. When I graduated I stayed on and worked there
and in other organisations for a year while I gained some
more qualifications and experience. I then decided to look
for full-time employment and found a job with an
educational charity that did personal development training
and made considerable use of outdoor activities in doing so.
I was able to use some of my qualifications and continue to
develop my skills in leadership and working with people. I

became a course director and stayed for five years until unfortunately the organisation had financial problems and had to make a large number of people redundant, including me.

'For the last 18 months I have been working as a freelance. I spent a fantastic summer in the Lake District and in Yorkshire, working in residential centres. There is more of a pattern to an instructor's work there. Normally I would spend time in preparation, then work with a group of eight to ten people for a period – or for a whole day. I would end by clearing up.'

Claudia is now back in Leicester, where several centres give her regular work, and she has just started to do some part-time lecturing on a BTEC National Diploma course in Outdoor Pursuits in a college of further education. She has a varied week. Yesterday, for instance, her morning was free although she had some BTEC paperwork to do. She spent the afternoon at the Tower Centre climbing wall. 'I have a group of ten people who come there for one session a week, plus some one-to-one coaching, and I also run a progressional course – for people who are booked in once a week to work towards a qualification.'

What does Claudia most enjoy in her work?
'I am passionate about outdoor education – especially in a wilderness environment. I want to encourage people to respect and enjoy the environment. I love working with both individuals and groups and seeing them achieve. It is brilliant to be able to combine all these things in one job.'

And are there any drawbacks?
'Yes. This work is not well paid! And training the way I did it can be expensive. If I had chosen to do it another way I could have saved myself some money. If I had started at the bottom in a full-time job in an outdoor education centre the employer would have helped with the cost of attending courses to gain certificates. I think, though, that for me, work in just one centre with similar customer groups every day would be very repetitive.'

Has she any advice for people hoping to become outdoor pursuits instructors?

'Yes. It's really important to get as much experience as possible. I don't mean simply in individual activities but in working with people. Unless you are doing one-to-one instruction when you are concentrating on technique – and even then communication skill is still important – you are spending most of your time in group work. People skills really are essential. Qualifications are important but employers want the right person more than certificates. They can always help you to get them and send on you courses if they wish.

'It's also important to really love the activities you want to qualify in. It's no good thinking "I suppose I should qualify in x" if you have no enthusiasm. Having said that, though, I do have one activity I'm less passionate about. I do basic archery – but only at work. All the other activities I also do as hobbies with friends in my free time.'

Claudia's qualifications include MLTB Mountain Leader Award, MLTB Single Pitch Award, BCU Level 2 Kayak Coach, Level 2 Canoe Coach, Level 1 Competition Canoe Polo Coach, GNAS Archery Leader, and Expedition First Aid. She has also completed a number of other relevant courses including the Level 1 Local Cave and Mine Leader training, the Institute of Outdoor Learning's Certificate of Professional Development (Teaching and Learning Styles), Developing Reviewing Skills, Neuro Linguistic Programming, Independent Psychological Service seminars (Defining Disaffection, Motivational Techniques, Social Competency, Complex Specific Learning Difficulties), Adventure for All – Disability Awareness, Personal Values in Youth Work Development, and a number of child protection and good practice courses. She continues to take advantage of voluntary work to develop her skills, especially with the British Mountaineering Council and Plas y Brenin (a large outdoor pursuits centre in Conwy).

PERSONAL TRAINER

In this role you would do the same sort of activities as a fitness instructor but, rather than taking classes, you'd work with one person at a time.

CHRISTIANNE WOLFF – PERSONAL TRAINER
Christianne's clients include film stars, pop stars, TV presenters, models and company directors. Among them are Pierce Brosnan, Dougray Scott (*Mission Impossible 2*), Martha Lane-Fox (founder of lastminute.com) – and many others whose names she can't reveal. (In this job discretion and maintaining client confidentiality are essential.)
She has an equally impressive list of qualifications – in aerobics, circuit training, body conditioning, indoor rock climbing, Khai Bo, marathon/triathlon, Pilates, weight lifting/training, yoga, spinning, pre- and post-natal exercise, step and exercise to music.

How did she begin?
'I am very fortunate in that I have been able to convert a barn owned by my parents and therefore have my own gym! I bought the equipment quite cheaply through eBay. There are some good bargains if you know what you are looking for and I now have a rower, treadmill, crosstrainer, parachute runner, barbells, steps and a bench.' But, she points out, it is not necessary to own all this equipment. Some personal trainers pay a fee to use a commercial gym when working with clients; others work in their clients' homes. When Christianne does home visits she carries only skipping ropes and Swiss balls in her car. Some of her clients have bought their own equipment. 'If they can afford to pay me they can also afford an exercise bike or other pieces of equipment.'

How does she decide on a programme for each client?
'At our first meeting I work through a questionnaire with them. I establish their past exercise history, get a medical history and ask what they hope to achieve and in what space of time. I do a fitness test, take blood pressure, test

fat/muscle ratio, and conduct a strength test. Then we knuckle down to setting goals. Do they want to improve general fitness? Lose weight? Train for a particular event? Are they being realistic? Some of my clients are high achievers and used to getting fast results! I have to explain that in this situation they'll have to compromise. I then draw up an exercise plan that includes work they will do with me and work to do on their own. I think this is important. Clients shouldn't get too dependent on me and need me there all the time.'

Some of her clients come through the website of the National Register of Personal Trainers, but the majority now hear of her by word of mouth. She also teaches four classes each week – and gets more individual clients or recommendations there.

Christianne has developed her career in several directions. She now spends most of her time working with individual clients, has her four weekly classes – and spends about 10% of her time writing on fitness topics. She is also about to launch, through her own website, a service for people who want to work with a personal trainer in their own homes, using a personally tailored programme.

'I was lucky when I qualified to land a part-time job at Pineapple Dance Studios in Covent Garden. It has a high profile and a lot of celebrities go there; consequently it is where media scouts tend to go if they are looking for a fitness expert. As a result a production company has asked me to present a fitness video and I have done some TV work.' She has also moved into fitness journalism – but through a more down-to-earth method. 'I was working in a health club one day when a reporter from the local paper came in looking for someone to write some articles for no payment. I had never written before, but I agreed to try. I had some articles published – then sent the cuttings to other magazines. This has brought me work from *M-Celebs*, the *Evening Standard Magazine*, *Health and Fitness*, and *Men's Fitness*.

You can find out more about Christianne's work at www.bodyrescue.net.

Christianne's experience is life at the top end. Many personal trainers are able to charge £60 per hour and more. Others earn around £30. And they do not enjoy the benefit of having their own gym.

THE DOWNSIDES

You would have to pay for your own training in order to get an approved qualification. (But you could do so part time while working in another job.)

You would need to allow for expenses like hire of space in a gym, *or* budget for your own car so that you could work in clients' homes.

Other expenses would include professional insurance and repairs to or replacement of equipment.

You would need to be able to handle money and to budget successfully. Most personal trainers also do some coaching or take classes – for which they are paid regularly.

You would work very unsocial hours.

PHYSICAL EDUCATION (PE) TEACHER

PE teachers are employed in schools and colleges in both the private and state sectors. In order to teach in the state sector teachers must have qualified teacher status. As teachers they usually have other duties in addition to teaching their main subject.

CLAIRE COOMER – PE TEACHER

Claire has been teaching at John Hanson Secondary (comprehensive) School in Andover, Hampshire, for two terms. Before starting this job she had a varied career.

Claire first did a degree in Sports Science at Brighton University. After leaving university, she decided to work for a master's degree in Sports Psychology and fund herself through working as a tennis coach. (She had qualified as a coach for this sport on her degree course.) It didn't work out, however. 'Somehow I seemed to take on more and more hours of coaching and the degree work got left behind! Eventually I became a full-time coach. I did that for two years – then worked in a leisure centre in Guildford where I worked as a tennis coach and a sports development officer.'

Claire then decided to teach. She was offered a job at her old college, where her skills were well known. It was a tertiary college – that is, a further education and sixth-form college combined – and since it catered for students over the statutory school-leaving age, it was not essential for her to be a qualified teacher. The college gave her time to study first for a City and Guilds Further Education Certificate, then a Certificate in Education in nearby Southampton. 'So I taught for four and a half days, doing about 19 hours of class contact time in my first two years. In my third year the teaching hours increased to 24 or 25.'

Claire had a varied timetable. She taught 16- to 19-year-old students doing A level Sports Studies, the college's own Sports Certificate course and GCSE Human Physiology, and some modules on the Intermediate GNVQ (General National Vocational Qualification, now replaced by Vocational GCSE) in Leisure and Tourism. There were a lot of different courses to prepare and it was hard work, especially as she was not a trained teacher. 'Seventy per cent of my work was teaching theory. Not being trained or having done teaching practice, I found it difficult to assess how much material I would cover in one lesson. There was a lot of marking to do too. I would work late, get up early and spend the whole of every half term week trying to get ahead.'

It was rewarding, though. 'The students had all chosen to come to college and to do the courses. They were all volunteers and all enthusiastic. They were not necessarily the most academic students in the college – or they might be doing two academic subjects and A level Sports Studies for pleasure. But they were so keen – and many went on to university to do sports courses.' As extra-curricular activities Claire ran the college ladies' football team (which became county champion) and also coached the men's football teams ('this was pretty rare'), indoor hockey and tennis. In her spare time (!) she coached juniors at the local tennis club.

The college decided to offer a two-year full-time BTEC National Diploma in Sports Studies – and Claire, still only in her third year of teaching, was appointed course leader. What did this involve?

'It meant a lot of paperwork and a lot of tracking! The students had to do a number of different modules, some of which I and the other two PE staff taught and some which were taught by staff from other departments. I actually had a course team of seven. I was so lucky in the other staff! We all knew each other well – and most of them did sport themselves. The maths lecturer was a tennis player, for example, and the biologist did a range of sports. It worked really well. We had a couple of formal meetings each term but we had lots of informal ones. I could say to Clare, who taught maths, for instance, that we had just done fitness assessments and produced an enormous amount of data which she could then use in the students' maths course. I could tell the IT lecturer (also a sportsman) that the students had to do a presentation for me – and he would teach them Powerpoint. It all integrated very well. The hardest subject the students had to do was science.

Unfortunately, some of it was rather dry – and some was quite difficult. Their biomechanics required knowledge of physics.'

Last year Claire left the college for a new job. 'The job was advertised. I could do it without leaving the area – and I felt it was time for a change. I had no school experience. I was not a qualified teacher for the statutory age group – and it was important to get QTS (Qualified Teacher Status) if I wanted to work abroad. I have two ambitions – one to do that master's degree in Sports Psychology (but this time on a full-time course) and the other to work in Australia at some point. I got the job at John Hanson and, because of my previous experience, have been able to qualify part-time through the Graduate Teaching Programme. My lessons to different year groups have been assessed and I am required to produce a portfolio of evidence that includes pieces of student work that I have marked and proof that I have liaised with parents, attended parents' evenings and written student reports and references.'

Work in a secondary school is very different from that in a tertiary college. For a start, the atmosphere is very different. 'From the moment the pupils arrive at 8.15am until they leave at 3.15pm it is non-stop. There is more structure to the day – and no free time at all. I have to register my tutor group twice a day and do break and lunch duty. The noise is incessant and bells go all the time.' Claire teaches much younger age groups – from 11- to 16-year-olds – and has a Year 10 tutor group (14- to 15-year-olds). She takes lessons in hockey, volleyball, badminton, orienteering, tennis, cricket, athletics, netball, rounders and football – in addition to teaching a junior sports leader award course, GCSE PE, and GCSE science with the top set. Except for the GCSE work all her classes are now practical. Next year she will be part of a team of staff teaching Personal and Social Education. 'I shall be covering health education – topics like drugs, drink, contraception and so on. I'm looking forward to it.'

PROFESSIONAL SPORTSPERSON

There are around 50,000 people employed in professional sport in the UK. Only a few very talented people make their living in team sports – mainly in football, cricket, basketball, rugby, ice hockey and hockey. Other sports that are played professionally include boxing, cycling, golf, motor racing, horse racing, snooker, show jumping, rugby and speedway riding. In some sports, people often turn professional in their teens, although in cricket some players wait until they are in their 20s to do so. (It is possible to have a full-time career in test and county cricket.) There are approximately 400 first-class cricketers under contract to 18 county clubs. There is also an England national side, made up of a small group of players who have central contracts with the England and Wales Cricket Board. The majority are between 18 and 35 year old.

A playing career is short and is usually over by the age of 40. Most professional players retire between the ages of 35 and 40, and many move into related careers such as coaching, journalism and sports management.

All professional players start playing their sport when they are young and work through the ranks of school teams, club and county teams, up to national level. In some sports – football is one – talent scouts and coaches visit sports events looking for young players with high potential. The age at which young people can start varies according to the sport. Boys can join football's Associated Schoolboy Scheme from 14, whereas cricketers and golfers often start in their early 20s. Tennis players are classed as adults at the age of 16. Professional sportspeople earn appearance fees and prize money. Famous players increase their income by advertising products.

Currently, there are more opportunities for men in professional sport than there are for women. This could change as more women are playing traditionally masculine sports like football. We could see more professional opportunities for women.

Golf is increasing in popularity in the UK, particularly among young people. More golf courses are being opened, so there is a growing demand for golf professionals. *Golf professional* is a confusing term, since there are actually two types of professional player. Tournament players play on the circuits and earn an income from prize money and sponsorship. To become tournament players, golfers must obtain a qualifying card. Competition is fierce. Professional golfers must be members of the Professional Golfers' Association (PGA). They have to pass exams and demonstrate high-level playing ability to be accepted.

Matt Stevens (see page 88) refers to his coach as a club professional. Club professionals are attached to a golf club. They help with administration, work in the golf shop, repair equipment, and may coach club members. There are around 2,200 club professionals in the UK. Around 30 are women.

FASCINATING FACT

- **Sports attract the biggest television audiences, led by the summer Olympics, World Cup football and Formula One racing.**

- **Football is the most attended or watched sport in the world.**

- **Paula Radcliffe is fluent in French and Italian and translates sports journals into English to keep her language skills up.**

- **Both Venus and Serena Williams studied fashion design at the Art Institute of Florida.**

- **For winning Wimbledon in 1968 Billie Jean King received £750. When she won Wimbledon for the first time in 2000, Venus Williams received £430,000.**

- **Ellen Macarthur has set up a trust to support and encourage young people who have cancer or leukaemia by taking them on sailing trips.**

- **Tiger Woods is the first player to win the Jack Nicklaus award for four consecutive years.**

RIDING INSTRUCTOR

Riding instructors teach a wide range of people at all levels from beginners to advanced.

They can work at riding schools, private stables, competition yards, colleges, polo yards and trekking centres. There are some freelance instructors who work on a self-employed basis at a number of centres. They must be able to ride well enough to demonstrate to pupils and must also have good communication and teaching skills.

Instructors usually qualify by taking the examinations of either the British Horse Society or the Association of British Riding Schools. These can be gained through an apprenticeship, through a full-time or part-time college course, or as a fee-paying student at a riding school.

SPORTS DEVELOPMENT WORK

People who used to play a sport but haven't done so for years may be looking for a way to get back into the game. Many sports clubs need help in starting up, recruiting new members, getting hold of grants and training their coaches. Many people would like to become coaches. Sports development officers make sure that as many people as possible are provided with the information and support that they need – whatever their sport.

KEVIN HARRIS – SPORTS DEVELOPMENT OFFICER (SDO), SOUTHAMPTON CITY COUNCIL
'SDOs' work varies according to their level of seniority and also according to how the work is organised in the authority they work for. There are three of us here – the Senior SDO who does more administrative and high-level work, another SDO who does general development work and also specialises in developing swimming – and myself. My remit is to develop coaching, and to provide information and advice to sports practitioners.

'So I have a very diverse role that includes anything from answering a simple phone enquiry about the whereabouts of tennis clubs, to helping community groups apply for funds, to running coaching education programmes. I work with teachers, sports coaches, sports clubs, individuals and groups across the city. I spend a major part of my time on advice concerned with fundraising. If a group of people want to start a club, for instance, I advise them which organisation to approach and help them with the application. The coaching education programme is very important. Coaches are volunteers, giving up their evenings and weekends. Without them many sporting activities would not happen. So it is essential to provide them support. I run monthly sessions for them in conjunction with a local higher education institution. I am also organising a special series of events for them this month as a Sports Coaches' Roadshow.

'I enjoy my job and count myself lucky to have found it. It does involve unsocial hours – I have to go to weekend coaching events and evening meetings. For example, I am going to one tonight with a community group that has got funding, with our help, to launch a football coaching programme for children in a deprived area. The hope is to give them something positive to do instead of hanging round the streets and potentially getting into trouble. But I can always have time off when other people are working.

'When I started my degree course I was unsure about a future career. In the second year I had the option of specialising in sports development or sport and recreation management. I chose sports development because I was interested in the sociological and cultural development aspects of sport. Eventually I decided that this was what I wanted to do.'

Kevin's Sports Coaches' Roadshow programme

Monday, 6–8pm:	Periodisation Workshop
Tuesday, 5.30–9.30pm:	Emergency Aid certificate
Thursday, 6.30–8.30pm:	Speed, Agility and Quickness (SAQ) taster session
Monday, 6.30–9.30pm:	Sports Coach UK Workshop – Injury prevention and management

> Wednesday, 6.30–9.30pm: Sport England Running Sport
> Workshop – Volunteer
> management
>
> Kevin's department has a website (www.southampton.gov.uk/
> Leisure/Sports), where you can learn more about his and his
> colleagues' work. It also has a Student Zone, which gives
> advice to people who would like to become sports
> development officers. Although it refers to opportunities in
> Southampton it contains useful information on getting into
> this career – and finding opportunities for voluntary work.
> You might find that your own local council has a similar
> website.

SWIMMING TEACHER

Swimming teachers give lessons to people who are learning how
to swim and to swimmers who are working for medals and
lifesaving awards. They might also coach swimmers for
competitions. Some of their lessons are given to groups; others to
individuals. They may go in the water with their pupils or instruct
from the side of the pool. Some swimming teachers are employed
by leisure centres and combine the work with that of a pool
attendant, lifeguard or leisure centre assistant. Others are self
employed.

YOGA TEACHER

Yoga teachers work mainly with classes and small groups,
although some may work with individuals. Some teachers place
greater emphasis on exercise and movement, while others
concentrate on breathing and meditation and the spiritual aspects
of yoga. Most work part time.

Training courses covering yoga therapy, anatomy, ethics and
practical yoga last from 18 to 30 days. Details of courses are
available from the Yoga Biomedical Trust (see Chapter 5).

OPPORTUNITIES TO WORK OVERSEAS

Once you have some qualifications under your belt you might want to spread your wings and see a bit of the world. Doing this could be a temporary thing – or you could even work abroad permanently. How?

Look at temporary and seasonal jobs for instructors in:

- hotels and campsites

- residential summer camps for children

- outdoor pursuits centres

- sailing schools

- water sports schools.

Fitness and exercise instructors can find work in centres within international hotel chains or in private clubs in many countries or on passenger cruise ships. Teachers can work in many countries – in British or international schools. There are a lot of sailing and water sports centres in other countries – and British qualifications are respected.

MEDIA JOBS RELATED TO SPORT

JOURNALIST

Very few journalists earn a living by writing about sport alone. Only national newspapers employ specialists. The majority of journalists are employed on local papers where they cover sport in addition to general news stories and other special interest topics. There are also opportunities to write for magazines – usually as a freelance.

There are different routes into careers in sports journalism. Some people first train as journalists, then become specialists in sport. Others develop expertise in a sport, or play professionally, then try their hand at writing and get into journalism that way.

- TV sports reporter Mike Bushell presents the sport on *News 24* and *BBC World* during the week and on BBC's *Breakfast* at the weekends. He has covered major events such as the Olympics and the World Cup. His background is in acting. He spent four years in the National Youth Theatre before doing a degree in theatre and television. However, his first full-time job was with a local newspaper. After jobs with two more papers he joined the BBC as a reporter with Radio Solent, before moving into television.

- Personal trainer Christianne Wolff accepted a request to write some articles on fitness for a newspaper – for no fee. She moved on to being able to charge for her work.

- Former professional cricketer David Gower writes on cricket for national newspapers.

PUBLIC RELATIONS

The definition of public relations, according to the Chartered Institute of Public Relations, is:

Public relations is about reputation – the result of what you do, what you say and what others say about you. Public relations is the discipline which looks after reputation, with the aim of earning understanding and support and influencing opinion and behaviour. It is the planned and sustained effort to establish and maintain goodwill and mutual understanding between an organisation and its publics.

Organisation can be a government body, a business, a profession, a public service or a body concerned with health, culture, education – indeed any corporate or voluntary body, large or small. *Publics* are audiences that are important to the organisation. They include customers – existing and potential;

employees and management; investors; media; government; suppliers; opinion-formers. *Understanding* is a two-way process. To be effective an organisation needs to listen to the opinions of those with whom it deals and not solely provide information. Issuing a barrage of propaganda is not enough in today's open society.'

Public relations professionals use a number of tools, including press releases, press conferences, dedicated media events and activities etc.

You will find much more information on public relations as a career in another book in this series, *Marketing and PR Uncovered*. What follows is a snapshot of some of the ways in which PR works with sport.

JOHNNY ABBOTT – PUBLIC RELATIONS PROFESSIONAL
Johnny Abbott, who has a degree in Public Relations from Bournemouth University, has worked in several PR industry sectors. One job as PR Manager for Gulf Air took him to Bahrain. Three of his jobs have been directly involved in sport.

'My first job after leaving university was with a marketing agency in Leicester called Rock Kitchen Harris, where I got my first taste of sport and community PR. I was involved in raising awareness of disabled athletes. Amongst the projects we managed was a major football initiative sponsored by BT, which had Gary Lineker as its patron. People with learning disabilities – even when their symptoms seem minor – have very limited opportunities to play football in an organised or structured environment. As part of the initiative, leagues and training days were set up around the country, along with major UK and European competitions. My role involved pre- and post-publicity of events, generating profiles of the sponsor's involvement, plus – and possibly most personally rewarding – raising awareness of the initiative's aims and how it was of real benefit to those who took part. We generated press, radio and television coverage from the events and used Gary Lineker's profile to highlight all the good work.'

After returning from the Middle East, Johnny worked for Limelight Projects, a specialist grassroots sports marketing and event management company. This was a temporary role working on 'back-office' participator support and administration for a major sporting event: Swimathon, the UK's largest participation swimming event. 'Finding work in sports PR and marketing is really competitive and it's not easy to walk straight into a plum job. This position was never going to be a permanent opportunity, but it was really important in that it helped me to maintain an involvement in sport while I continued to look. Plus, I gained a range of new experiences and valuable contacts, which is always important in this industry.'

Soon Johnny successfully landed a role at Karen Earl Sponsorship (KES), one of Europe's leading specialist sponsorship consultancies.

KES advises major brands such as Coca-Cola, British Airways, Guinness and RBS on national, European and global sponsorships in sports, entertainment and the arts. One of the events Johnny worked on related to the Athens Olympic Games.

'UK Online was the official internet services provider [ISP] of the UK Olympics team, so I was responsible for the PR of this sponsorship and ensuring UK Online gained visibility for their association amongst the target audiences – which were primarily their potential customers.

'This was really tough as UK Online had to compete for Olympic coverage against much bigger brand sponsors. Also, the link between an ISP and the Olympics was tenuous and there was no budget for high-profile athletes to help draw attention to the company. In these circumstances you have to be creative and work hard in creating newsworthy stories that can secure coverage for your client. We succeeded by working with little-known athletes who we gambled would be big news nearer the Olympics or had a wider human interest. We hit gold when we created media events involving a track cyclist who had won lots of medals, a fencer whose coach had escaped his native Eastern European country and had subsequently been involved in a Bond movie, plus a gymnast called Beth Tweddle – who was to become Great Britain's most successful athlete. With Beth, we organised a "One hundred days countdown to the Olympics", where she performed at the British Science Museum. This was covered by five television crews.

'In principle sports PR is no different from any other PR – but in my case I just found it more interesting. Simply, it's about communicating and engaging with a specific target audience though the use of the media, plus any range of events and activities. I think to be successful you must be creative, but also be a good communicator and very tenacious. Like sport itself, it's a very competitive business, but, equally, can almost be just as rewarding.'

SPORTS PHOTOGRAPHER

As with journalism, it is usual to qualify first as a photographer, then specialise. Photographers may be employed by one newspaper, by an agency that submits pictures to a number of papers or be freelance. It is possible to train in general photography, or to do a specialist training course in press photography which is recognised by the National Council for the Training of Journalists.

MEDICAL WORK RELATED TO SPORT AND FITNESS

NUTRITIONIST

Some people take short qualifications in nutrition and diet for a healthy lifestyle and use them in their work as coaches or trainers. There is also a much longer training course – a degree – which leads to work as a nutritionist or dietician with people who have all kinds of illnesses and dietary problems.

OSTEOPATH

Osteopaths treat injuries by manipulating bones and joints. It is not possible to train purely as a sports osteopath. A full-time course must be taken first.

The entry qualifications, training and work of an osteopath are described fully in another book published by Trotman, *Getting Into Healthcare Professions*.

SPORT AND EXERCISE SCIENTIST/ PHYSIOLOGIST

Performers and coaches sometimes employ sport and exercise scientists who use their specialist training to improve aspects of training and reduce the risk of injury. They might also suggest adjustments to training programmes or changes of equipment. They often work as freelance consultants.

SPORTS PHYSIOTHERAPIST

Sports physiotherapists treat a wide range of sport-related injuries and strains. They use a range of treatments, including manipulation, massage, heat treatment, therapeutic exercise, electrotherapy, ultrasound, acupuncture and hydrotherapy.

Some sports physiotherapists work only with professional sportspeople. (There are some full-time opportunities in professional sport – but many physiotherapists who work with sports teams are volunteers.) Others work with amateur sportspeople and people who take part in sport as a leisure activity. Many of those who hold sports injuries clinics are either self employed or are already employed in hospitals and do sessions in leisure and recreation centres. The increasing interest

in sport is leading to more opportunities for sports
physiotherapists.

It is not possible to train solely for sports physiotherapy. You
would have to qualify first in general physiotherapy – which is a
much broader profession. This means taking a physiotherapy
degree approved by the Health Professions Council. During your
training you would treat all kinds of patients in clinics and on
wards. You would have to be prepared to help some cough up
fluid from their lungs after operations and to coax reluctant ones
out of bed to exercise after hip operations or similar.

GILL DRIVER – PHYSIOTHERAPIST

Gill works in Winchester, Hampshire. She works for three
days a week in a clinic at the city's leisure centre and spends
one day teaching physiotherapy students at Southampton
University. She also has two children. Gill did her degree
course at Queen Elizabeth Hospital, Birmingham, then moved
to Southampton General Hospital, where she gained
experience in different specialities – orthopaedics,
neurosurgery, intensive care, cardiothoracic, paediatrics and
work with the elderly – before moving to the gym (where she
treated lower limbs), then to hydrotherapy, and the treatment
room, treating spines, backs, necks and shoulders. Next
came a move to Bournemouth to gain experience in GP
practices. She could have gone on to specialise in any of
those areas and made a career in the NHS, but she had
decided by this point that she wanted to work in private
practice and to specialise in sports injuries work.

'While I was in Bournemouth I did some sports injury and
other private work in the evenings. On moving to Winchester
I worked for 18 hours a week in the NHS – and at the same
time worked part time for a friend who had a private
practice. I also began to work here. It was hard work! You
cannot just walk into private practice. You have to build up
the work gradually and keep your main job until you are
confident that you can go it alone. When I started, if patients
wanted appointments on a Saturday afternoon, they got

them. I couldn't turn any away. I was working from 7am until 9pm on many days.

'Now, I work with four other physiotherapists, all of whom do a certain number of sessions here and have other jobs too. We are completely independent and are not employed by the leisure centre. We rent the rooms (treatment room and office) and have bought all the equipment ourselves. Only one of us is here at a time but we do communicate by phone and meet occasionally. We used to do all our own administration but have just taken someone on to do that so that we can concentrate on patient care. Between us we keep the clinic open from 9am to 5pm and from 6pm to 8pm.

'Anyone who wants private physiotherapy can consult us; they do not have to be suffering from sports injuries. I would say that about half my patients have sports injuries and the remainder come with all kinds of problems. I regularly use the whole range of treatments and give re-education and exercise advice.

'Patients come by GP referral or by word of mouth, and many come simply because we are in the sports centre. They sometimes come in hesitantly and explain that their problem is not sport-related. The patients I see who do have sports injuries come with a number of different problems, including strains or damage to tendons, muscles, ligaments and cartilage. They might have injured themselves on a sports court or pitch or they may come because they are suffering from an injury that affects their ability to do sport. They might notice pain from a previous injury or condition that makes an exercise class painful, for instance. I see a lot of people with back and neck problems and posture-related pain.

'I love my job and feel that I have the best of both worlds. I can work just as hard as I choose to. I can fit my work around collecting the children from school. Very important to me is the fact that I am still using all my skills and am still "hands on". As you move up the ladder in general physiotherapy you have more management and administrative work to do and less patient contact. I still have that. There are other satisfactions. I can spend as long as I need to with each patient. In an NHS hospital they would only be able to have a certain number of sessions. And we do not have waiting lists. We can usually offer appointments on the same day that someone makes a request.

'There are drawbacks, of course. I have no paid holidays or sick leave. If I were ill I would have no cover whereas in a hospital someone else would pick up some of the cases. I can't be ill. Patients expect me to be here! I have to pay for my own continuing professional development. My professional association, the Organisation for Chartered Physiotherapists in Private Practice, requires members to spend 25 hours a year in training and updating skills. If I worked in a hospital this would be paid for. A possible downside could be professional isolation because I am not working with colleagues every day. But I do have my day a week at the university and can exchange ideas and discuss cases with colleagues there.

'Other than the technical skills, communication is the most important. We have to be able to establish relationships with patients and their relatives. We work with patients of all ages and we also have to build working relationships with doctors and consultants.'

SPORTS PSYCHOLOGIST

Sports psychologists help amateur and professional players improve their performance through the use of psychological techniques. Teachers, coaches and personal trainers all use psychology in their work. Opportunities to work purely as a sports psychologist are limited: although there are some people who earn a living from this work alone, many others are also teachers, lecturers or researchers, or work in a combination of all these jobs. A major part of the work is concerned with trying to improve a team's or an individual performer's motivation.

KIERAN KINGSTON – SPORTS PSYCHOLOGIST

'The value of psychology in sport is increasingly recognised – but even so there are limited opportunities for sports psychologists to practise as full-time consultants. I have colleagues who work full time but most, like myself, do a combination of this and other work in sports psychology, such as teaching or research. I do all three. I am a senior lecturer in sports psychology at the University of Wales Institute, Cardiff, I am involved in a number of ongoing research projects and, when time permits, I work with groups and individuals as a sports psychologist. My main focus in this work is with elite golfers – both professional and amateur – and with professional snooker players. My clients come from different sources – referrals from colleagues, from golf clubs (I play locally), from the BASES (British Association for Sport and Exercise Science) register, which can be consulted by anyone who is looking for a sports psychologist, and most of all through word of mouth.

'In my opinion, the principal role of sports psychologists is to provide players with tools to help them perform better. It can involve facilitating the development of strategies to help them become more effective when training or competing or involve mental preparation and development of competition plans. Much of the work is what we call 'Band Aid' – that is, a player will come with a specific problem. For example, a professional athlete might seek out my support to deal with nerves in competition that are undermining his/her performance. Initially, I am seeking to gather information. What are the triggers to the occurrence of the nervous reaction? How long have they been occurring? How does this state differ from when he/she performs well? What (if anything) is done differently before situations when the nerves cause performance to drop, as opposed to when they do not get in the way? I am trying to start to understand the nature of the condition and the underlying causes; the athlete will also (I hope) come to develop a greater self-awareness, which in itself can serve as the start of the therapeutic process. Once we are both comfortable that we are starting to understand and even rationalise the causes, I will work on strategies to alleviate the issue.

'An important part of a sports psychologist's work is to establish a relationship with a client and to look holistically at the problem that presents. Does the player have problems outside sport and need support in other areas, for instance? You must be able to make them feel comfortable with you and ready to open up. It may also be the case that the issues are beyond your area of expertise (in which case you might refer the athlete to another professional such as a clinical psychologist). Recognising and accepting your own limitations is an important aspect of the consultancy role.

'Work with groups is different. I do seminars and workshops for small groups of sports bursary students at Cardiff University. Here, I take on more of an educational role and do not concentrate on any specific problems. Again, my role is to help these athletes acquire skills to assist their performance. I am also contracted to the PGA for whom I also do workshops and lectures – for elite coaches and registered professional players. I have just returned from giving a series of workshops in Edinburgh.'

SPORTS THERAPIST

Sports therapists treat injuries and also assess risks and advise on how to avoid injury. They might, for instance, play a role in training by assessing possible weaknesses and recommending ways to prevent them developing. Some also advise on nutrition. Some of their work is therefore similar to that of physiotherapists who specialise in sports-related work.

The usual way into the job is to take a degree or diploma in sports therapy, which will include subjects like anatomy, biomechanics, nutrition, physiology, rehabilitation (including massage and electrotherapy) and sports psychology.

There are openings in sports injury clinics, or with professional teams, sports clubs, health and fitness clubs/gyms, sports and leisure centres and with a number of NHS Trusts that employ sports therapists for rehabilitation work. Many sports therapists are either self-employed or have two or more part-time jobs.

Currently, sports therapy is not a state-registered profession and anyone may use the title 'Sports Therapist' (although there are proposals to introduce a system of approved professional registration). The best way to find a suitable course is to look for one that is accredited by the Society of Sports Therapists.

The type and range of treatments that an individual therapist is qualified to offer and can be insured to offer will depend upon which course they have taken.

How do I get into sport and fitness?

It all depends on what stage you are at right now. There is more than one way of getting into most jobs, and jobs in sport and fitness are no exception. You can nearly always find your way into a career area whether you leave school at 16 or 18 year olds or go on to higher education. Having said that, however, a career in professional sport does require you to have made an early start – playing for amateur teams, competing in events etc.

HOW THEY STARTED

'I didn't really enjoy school all that much and left after the first year of A levels. I found an Advanced Apprenticeship placement myself at Ipswich Town Football Club and worked on a programme called Community Challenge. I did some coaching and helped to teach basic life skills – and really enjoyed both.'

Andy Crump, former Apprentice

ADAM DODD – LEISURE ASSISTANT

Adam obtained an Advanced GNVQ (now Applied A level) in Leisure and Tourism at sixth-form college. He originally wanted a career as a hotel manager, and worked part time at the Belfry Hotel in Sutton Coldfield to gain experience during his studies. Unfortunately they didn't have a full-time position for him when he left college but Adam had by then become interested in the leisure side of things and had completed his lifesaving qualification. He applied for the position of leisure assistant and was successful. He has now been working as a leisure assistant for four years.

Although the interview for the position itself was fairly informal, Adam had to demonstrate his knowledge and skills in several areas, including swimming two lengths in under a minute, and demonstrating his first aid knowledge. It was also essential that he had his NPLQ (National Pool Lifeguard Qualification), as lifeguard work forms a large part of his responsibilities.

JOHN LEDGWIDGE – APPRENTICE

John left school with 10 GCSE grades A and B but instead of entering the sixth form or attending college full time, he opted to live out his lifelong dream. When he was 13 years old he had set his heart on becoming a groundskeeper, and he successfully gained an apprenticeship at Coventry City Football Club by writing direct to the club. Although he was only 16 years old, he had already been working as a volunteer at City for the past two years, so the head groundskeeper decided to give him the opportunity to train as an Apprentice.

KEVIN HARRIS – SPORTS DEVELOPMENT OFFICER

Kevin has a degree in Sports Studies from the University of Chichester. During the course he was able to take a sports development pathway. Like many other people in this book he discovered that the way into the job he wanted involved gaining experience through voluntary work. It also involved hard graft! At one stage he was working 39 hours a week in a full-time job and further hours as a volunteer.

'I soon found that you don't leave university and just walk into a job! It hit me that I needed a lot more experience and that voluntary work was the way to get it. I took a full-time clerical job selling membership of fitness clubs, and contacted this department to see if I could come in and help out on a voluntary basis. The hours in my full-time job were flexible, so I was able to juggle them over a 39-hour week and come in here to do some of the administrative work and help out with projects.

'I had gained football coaching qualifications on my degree course – so I also applied for some paid coaching jobs. I got a position with Southampton City Football Club, coaching on their Football in the Community Programme. I worked all over the city, bringing quality coaching to children in after-school clubs in primary schools and in a sports centre on Saturdays. I also coached my girlfriend's brother's football team (13-year-olds) on a voluntary basis. Looking back, I don't know how I fitted it all in! But I cannot stress enough the importance of doing work like this if you want to get into my job.'

Kevin increased his activities during the summer holidays, working weekends with the Hampshire and Isle of Wight Partnership Active Sports Programme, as a development officer for women's and girls' football – 'I had never coached girls before, so it was a new experience' – and on a rugby community project, both of which gave him real sport development experience, and he worked for the same partnership at the Hampshire Youth Games. 'This event takes place every year and allows young people to take part in a variety of sports – girls' football, rugby, basketball and so on. There were also the Parallel Games for young people with disabilities. I ran a disabled players' football tournament.'

All this work gave Kevin experience – but equally valuable was the opportunity to network. He got to know sports development officers and his work became known. So when a vacancy for a sports development officer came up with the city council he applied for a job which he already knew and understood. Ironically, at this point Kevin had applied for and been accepted to do a master's degree in Sport on Wednesday afternoons. He managed to convince the interviewers that it would be good for the department if he gained this qualification – and was allowed to do so, provided that he worked his full week of 37.5 hours. So once again Kevin is doing more than one job.

SUE HORNIBROOK – ASSISTANT MANAGER, PRIVATE HEALTH CLUB

Sue has always been interested in sport and is a qualified gymnastics coach. When she left school, however, she became a receptionist with a computer company.

'Office work was not enough for me. I enjoyed the work but wanted to do the same job in an environment that interested me more. When Bannatyne's opened I came here as a receptionist. I was promoted to reception manager at the club in Durham – then when an opening became available, came back here to manage reception. The manager saw that I was keen to progress and offered to let me do the assistant manager training course. Then, while I was still doing it, the job became vacant. I applied and was successful.'

GILL DRIVER – PHYSIOTHERAPIST

Gill started out by training as a physiotherapist and working in the NHS. She then set up her private practice by working evenings and weekends in sports injury work. When she had enough private work she left the NHS.

CLAUDIA SARNER – OUTDOOR PURSUITS INSTRUCTOR

'I did voluntary work with young people – scouting and Duke of Edinburgh's Award work in the university vacations. I also gained some qualifications in particular activities. As a result I was able to do some paid work in outdoor pursuits as well.' She then continued to gain experience while working for different employers and gained more specialist qualifications to increase her employability.

KIERAN KINGSTON – SPORTS PSYCHOLOGIST

'My first step was to do a degree in Physical Education at University of Wales, Bangor, with the aim of becoming a PE teacher. I became interested in sports psychology during my second year when we did some modules in the subject and went on to do my third year project on 'Focus of attention while executing a sport skill'. I then decided that I wanted a career consisting of teaching, research and work with athletes. My first step was to enrol on a research-based part-time master's degree in Sports Psychology – funded through part-time teaching.

'As a result of a presentation I made I was invited to the University of North Carolina as a visiting scholar. At the time, I was undecided on whether I wanted to pursue a doctorate (to be honest, it always seemed like something that intellectuals got involved with, and I never did, and still don't, view myself in that manner). However, by the time I returned from the USA I had decided that I wanted to continue and develop my research ideas, and attempt to complete a PhD. While doing all my academic work I did the BASES [British Association for Sport and Exercise Science] qualifications in sports psychology, which involved getting a minimum of three years' supervised experience working with different athletes. After combining my doctoral studies with a full-time teaching job I moved to a university teaching position at Liverpool for one year, and then came to Cardiff.'

AND SOME CELEBRITIES

● Paula Radcliffe started running at the age of 7 when she ran for one mile with her father, a marathon runner. Aged 9, she joined Bedford Athletics Club. In her first national race as a schoolgirl, she came in 299th! But she believed that if she persisted she could do it in the end. She trained hard, entered events – and never gave up. She put up with comments about being the person who always finished just outside the medals – and went on to win the London Marathon at her first attempt. In the same year she became the European 10,000 metres champion and won the Commonwealth 5,000 metres. She still has the coach she met at the Bedford Club.

- BBC presenter Sue Thearle began her career on a local newspaper before moving to the *Daily Telegraph*, where she worked as a football writer. Sue is a presenter on BBC's *News 24*, *Grandstand* and *Match of the Day* – where she is the only woman.

- Venus and Serena Williams started winning tennis tournaments when they were ten years old. Everyone knows that they trained on public courts, coached by their father. They had professional coaching at one point, but then returned to their father, who continued to coach them and to manage their careers. He insisted that they both finish high school rather than concentrate on their junior tennis circuit – and both went on to art school.

- Ellen Macarthur was inspired by sailing trips she made with her aunt when she was 8 years old. She saved up for three years to buy her first boat, which was an 8ft dinghy. She sailed around Britain on her own when she was 18 years old. Sailors need equipment (a boat, obviously!) and sponsorship. Ellen lived for three years in a Portakabin while saving to buy a Classe Min Yacht and raise sponsorship to compete in a transatlantic race.

- Jonny Wilkinson was inspired by his father, a rugby player, who took him to Farnham Minis when he was 5 years old. He was hooked immediately. He never gave any other career a serious thought. He knew he wanted to be a rugby professional – and turned down a university place in order to sign a two-year contract with Newcastle. Today, he is apparently always the first one on to the training field and the last one off!

Do these stars demonstrate determination, or what?

WHAT ARE YOU GOING TO DO?

Here is a selection of different entry routes.

APPRENTICESHIPS
These are available in:

- sports and recreation

- the horse industry.

You can find out which ones might be available in your area from your Connexions personal adviser or careers adviser.

Apprenticeships (England) and Foundation Apprenticeships (Wales) are for anyone 16 to 24 years old who has left full-time education and has not yet found work or for people in the same age range who are already in employment. There is no set time limit for completing an apprenticeship but all programmes last at least 12 months. Most people enter them at 16 or 17 years old but some take further qualifications first. There is a second programme – Advanced Apprenticeship in England or Modern Apprenticeship in Wales – that lasts at least 24 months.

Most apprentices are counted as employees and are paid a wage (the going rate for the job). A small number are linked to a training provider and are paid a minimum allowance. The majority of employers now offer more than the minimum.

Modern Apprentices follow a training programme consisting of work experience and training for their jobs. They achieve National Vocational Qualification (NVQ) at Level 2, Key Skills and a Technical Certificate. When they complete the programme, they might decide to progress to an Advanced or Modern Apprenticeship.

Apprenticeships and Foundation Apprenticeships train people up to NVQ Level 3 and is for people who are aiming to work at supervisory or management level. They are intended for 16- and 17-year-old school and college leavers with the ability to gain high-level skills and qualifications. Some people, however, start programmes after doing A levels when they are 18 years old.

In Scotland, programmes are known as Modern Apprenticeships through Skillseekers.

t's been a big success for me, as I've now got a ull-time job here and have almost completed my NVQ at Level 2 in Sport and Recreation. The pprenticeship really worked for me as I could do a ob I really enjoyed at the same time as gaining ualifications – and now I have just been appointed full-time football development officer at the Club.

My job involves helping to run our Community Youth ootball League and coaching young people taking art in our holiday coaching and weekly coaching rogrammes. I love my job.'

Andy Crump, former Apprentice

CLAIRE BRYANT – APPRENTICE
Claire has always had an interest in sports and recreation. She left school with nine GCSE passes and two A levels (Physical Education and Business Studies) and enrolled on an Advanced Apprenticeship programme in Sport and Recreation at Guildford Leisure Complex, which has over 3 million visitors and has a range of facilities including athletics track, ice rink, leisure pool, competition swimming pool, ten pin bowling and health and fitness centre.

Claire currently holds the position of Health Suite Supervisor. She has already completed four NVQ units at Levels 3 and 4, Key Skills, and job-related qualifications including Sports Leader Award, Premier Fitness Instructor, Nutrition and Exercise Certificate (NHS) and First Aid at Work.

She has had to do assignments as part of her NVQ work – and three of these, 'Supporting the Efficient Use of Resources', 'Creating Effective Working Relations' and

'Maintaining Sport and Recreation Equipment and Facilities', have been acknowledged by her manager as contributing to the success of the business. In fact, Claire is regarded by members of senior management as such a strong member of staff that she has recently been seconded to the personnel section of the organisation to carry out project work.

Her ambition after completing her apprenticeship is to set up a personal training business and then to train as a PE teacher. She hopes to start a PE degree in three years' time.

JOHN LEDGWIDGE – APPRENTICE (PITCH), COVENTRY CITY FOOTBALL CLUB

'I chose this route because an apprenticeship offers practical work experience, training and a wage. Being a lifelong Sky Blues fan I always wanted to walk on the pitch and play for the team, but after I broke my arm when playing in goal when I was 13 years old, I decided the best option was to try and become a groundskeeper, and that way I could walk on the pitch every day.

'Over the past year I have spent one day a week attending Warwickshire College, at Moreton Morell, working towards an NVQ in Horticulture. I was able to learn every aspect of groundkeeping, maintaining the pitch to Premier League standards. I have now completed my apprenticeship, and to celebrate the start of the new football season I will soon be working towards the Advanced Apprenticeship in Amenity Horticulture.'

John is hoping to be soon managing the grounds at the new Sky Blues Academy, looking after seven pitches, including four made from grass, two indoor pitches and one artificial surface.

NVQS

National Vocational Qualifications are awarded in England and Wales; in Scotland the equivalent is Scottish Vocational

Qualifications. They are work-related qualifications that demonstrate what a person is capable of doing, and are available at five levels, ranging from Level 1, designed for new entrants to a career, right up to Level 5, which equates to postgraduate level. You don't gain S/NVQs by taking exams but by being assessed at work on how well you perform set tasks. You record your achievements in a *portfolio of evidence* and get a manager or supervisor to sign each one.

Examples of S/NVQs on offer in sport include:

● Sport, Recreation and Allied Occupations

● Sport, Recreation and Allied Occupations (Activity Leadership)

● Sport, Recreation and Allied Occupations (Teaching and Instructing)

● Sport, Recreation and Allied Occupations (Operational Services)

● Sport, Recreation and Allied Occupations (Operations and Development)

● Outdoor Education, Development Training, Recreation

● Spectator Safety

● Achieving Excellence in Sports Performance.

In fitness you could gain an S/NVQ in Instructing Exercise and Fitness.

OTHER INDUSTRY-RELATED QUALIFICATIONS

In the fitness industry it is really, really important to take qualifications that employers (and insurance companies) recognise. Also, the customers want to know that they are being taught or trained by people who know what they are doing! You'll probably have to pay to do these – unless an employer will help out. So you need to know that you are getting value for money. There are some dodgy outfits willing to take your cash and offer imposing certificates. Always make sure that training courses are recognised. (You can check with the Register of Exercise Professionals.)

Highly respected qualifications are:

● YMCA Fitness Industry Training

● Oxford, Cambridge and RSA

● Institute for Sport, Parks and Leisure (ISPAL).

YMCA FITNESS INDUSTRY TRAINING
This offers a large number of courses, most on a modular basis. You can take each module individually and at your own pace or follow intensive daytime courses, evening classes or weekend courses. Module titles include:

● Advanced Gym Instruction

● Anatomy and Physiology

● Aqua Training

● Body Conditioning

● Business and Marketing for the Fitness Professional

● Circuit Training

● Client Lifestyle and Fitness Assessment

● Components and Principles of Fitness

● Exercise Nutrition

● Exercise Technique and Training Methods

● First Aid at Work

● Fitness Instruction

- Gym Inductions

- Gym Instruction

- Health and Safety in Exercise

- Training in Different Environments.

By taking a set combination of modules you could achieve one of the following awards.

- Personal Trainer Award, which can be studied over 45 days or module by module.

- Gym Instructor Award, which would take 13 days full time plus a one-day assessment. Again, a modular method is also available.

- Studio Instructor Award, which would take 13 days full time plus a one-day assessment, or module by module.

A Diploma in Sports Massage is also available.

OXFORD, CAMBRIDGE AND RSA
These offer awards in:

- aqua

- circuits

- exercise to music

- gym

- step.

INSTITUTE FOR SPORT, PARKS AND LEISURE (ISPAL)
In sport you can qualify by completing courses offered by ISPAL. The institute offers qualifications and membership to people working in the wider leisure industry. It is in the process of revising its qualifications and the revised courses will be available

soon. For anyone already enrolled on a course it will also continue to offer the former ILAM qualifications.

For sport and recreation you could choose from the qualifications included in the Institute's Professional Qualification Scheme:

NVQ	ISPAL equivalent
Level 5	Advanced Diploma in Leisure Management
Level 4	Diploma in Leisure Management
Level 3/4	Certificate in Leisure Management
Level 3	Duty Manager Award
	GP Referral Course
Level 2/3	Certificate in Leisure Operations
	Certificate in Technical Operations
Level 2	First Award
	NARS (National Aquatic Rescue Standard)
	Leisure Assistant Award

ISPAL also offers:

● Certificate in Technical Operations (Pool Plant Operators)

● Continuing Professional Development programme.

FULL-TIME COURSES

If you are now in Year 11 and are planning to stay on into your school's sixth form or transfer to a sixth-form college or college of further education you could take:

● AS and/or A level in Physical Education

● AS and/or A level Sport and Physical Education

● BTEC National Diploma in Sport and Exercise Science.

A LEVELS

Following are descriptions of the two A level courses, taken from the prospectus for Queen Elizabeth Sixth-Form College in Darlington (www.qeliz.ac.uk).

Physical Education
This course studies the demands made upon a sports performer from physiological, psychological and sociological points of view. It offers students the opportunity to demonstrate their understanding and personal competence in two activities and students are expected to be actually involved in the activities throughout the course.

This practical element involves:

● personal competence in two sports

● ability to identify and correct faults

● ability to demonstrate specified skills and techniques in a competition situation

● development of a fitness plan in one practical activity which is recorded in a personal performance portfolio and must be put into practice by candidates.

Two modules involve students gaining knowledge of anatomy and applying it to sport activities. As well as the body working, it also involves knowledge of the mind and skill acquisition that leads into sports psychology.

Two modules study contemporary issues in society and compare our sporting policies with those of the USA, Australia and France.

Course content
Unit 1: Anatomy: movement analysis including bones, muscles and joints. Heart and circulation. Respiration. Skill Acquisition: learning and developing skilful movement

Unit 2: Contemporary Studies: issues connected with sport in society

Unit 3: Practical and Personal Performance Portfolio

Unit 4: Sports Psychology and History of Sport

Unit 5: Exercise Physiology: energy, training, enhancing sports performance, extended synoptic essay

Unit 6: Practical Training Plan and individual coaching knowledge which is assessed in an oral examination.

Teaching methods
30% practical at AS, 15% at A2.

The AS personal performance portfolio is an extended piece of work continually assessed throughout the year.

Units 1, 2, 4 and 5 are teacher-led using a combination of styles and practical examples to demonstrate theoretical issues.

Students regularly complete exam-style tasks and questions.

In order to study PE at A level, a student should perform at school 'first team' standard in at least one sport and be a club member to continue one sport for the duration of the course.

Sport and Physical Education

This course studies the demands made upon a sports performer from physiological, psychological and sociological points of view. It follows the historical evolution of sport in this country and the part that it plays within our current society and comparisons with the USA and France are then made.

At AS level there is assessment of personal performance in a personal exercise programme and a project that involves students observing and analysing performance. This is continued at A2 in an extended assignment where students apply concepts, theories and models from psychology, physiology and biomechanics in analysing the problems of improving the sports performance for themselves or for another athlete.

Course content
Unit 1: Anatomy: movement analysis including bones, muscles and joints. Heart and circulation. Respiration. Skill Acquisition: learning and developing skilful movement

Unit 2: Contemporary Studies: issues connected with sport in society and history of sport

Unit 3: Practical and Personal Exercise Plan – involves students devising and implementing a six-week fitness plan. Project: involves students observing and analysing performance

Unit 4: Exercise Physiology, Biomechanics and Sports Psychology

Unit 5: Factors which affect the development of an elite athlete, includes media, sponsorship, hooliganism, Olympic and World Games

Unit 6: Written Project Investigation and an extended assignment.

Teaching methods
30% practical at AS, 15% at A2.

The AS personal exercise plan is an extended piece of work that involves practical fitness aspects.

Units 1, 2, 4 and 5 are teacher-led using a combination of styles and practical examples to demonstrate theoretical issues.

Units 3 and 6 involve students in research, observation and analysis as well as individual project work.

BTEC NATIONAL DIPLOMA IN SPORT AND EXERCISE SCIENCES
On this programme you would take six core units and 12 specialist units.

The core units are:

● Exercise Physiology

● Practical Sports Coaching

● Scientific Principles for Sport and Exercise

● Skill Acquisition

● Sport and Exercise Psychology

● Sport and Exercise Sciences Project.

Compulsory specialist units are:

- Anatomy for Sport and Exercise

- Nutrition for Sport and Exercise.

You would choose optional specialist units from:

- Biomechanics

- Exercise, Health and Lifestyle

- Fitness Testing

- Physiological Factors in Sport and Exercise

- Practical Sport Performance

- Qualitative Sport and Exercise Research

- Quantitative Sport and Exercise Research

- Social Aspects of Sport

- Sport Industry Experience

- Sport Massage

- Sports Injuries

- Technological Developments in Sport.

Any of the full-time courses already discussed could be used as a stepping stone to a higher education course.

HIGHER NATIONAL DIPLOMA (HND) COURSES

HNDs are two-year courses (full time) or three years (sandwich) which have an entry requirement of one A level/two Highers or S/NVQ Level 3. You can also offer approved equivalent qualifications and experience at the discretion of universities and colleges. The A level need not be a vocational one: almost any subject is accepted.

Colleges and universities offering HND courses are free to design their own programmes, so content can vary considerably. They do however receive guidelines from either Edexcel (formerly the Business and Technology Education Council) or SQA, the Scottish Qualifications Authority. These are two validating bodies that monitor the quality of courses and award the diploma.

Content of a typical Higher National Diploma course in Leisure Management:

● Business Law

● Business Strategy

● Business Systems in Leisure

● Customer Care and Service Quality

● Leisure Organisations and Issues

● Management of People

● Managing Finance

● Marketing and Sales

● Operations Management of Sport and Leisure

● Sports and Leisure Marketing

● Options: Events Management Pathway, Outdoor Recreation, Sports and Leisure Management.

FOUNDATION DEGREES

These programmes are not unlike HNDs in content – and the Department for Education and Skills expects all HND programmes to become foundation degrees in due course. Two major differences at the moment are that foundation degree programmes are drawn up by the universities and colleges that run them and not by BTEC, and they must contain work experience.

If you did a foundation degree you would have the option of entering employment and continuing training there, or of converting the qualification into an honours degree through further study, usually by transfer into the second or third year of a related degree course.

DEGREE COURSES

Most degree courses last three years; a few take a year longer and include a year's work experience placement. Entry requirement are either two A levels/three Highers or equivalent (for example National Diplomas or NVQ/SVQ Level 3). Other qualifications and experience are sometimes accepted. Entry grades vary in different institutions – not always because some courses are better than others but because popular universities and college can ask for higher grades!

Content of a typical first degree course in Sports Science:

- Applied Coaching Science

- Basic and Applied Sports Science

- Biomedical Implications of Exercise

- Functional Anatomy

- Fundamentals of Human Nutrition

- Human Physiology

- Measurement and Evaluation of Human Performance

- Metabolic Nutrition

- Metabolism and Endocrinology

- Muscle Function

- Paediatric and Geriatric Exercise Science

- Physical Performance Assessment

- Sensory and Motor Physiology

- Sociological Issues in Sport

- Sports Psychology.

A degree course in Physical Education with Qualified Teacher Status would typically involve:

- Child Development and Learning

- Information and Communication Technology

- Personal and Social Education

- Physical Activities

- Physical Education

- School and Community Partnerships

- School Experience

- The Teacher as a Professional

- Options in: Coaching, Dance, Games, Gymnastics, Health Focused Studies, Leisure Studies, Special Needs.

Some degree and/or diploma programmes that are available:

- Applied Sports Science

- Coach Education and Sports Development

- Exercise Physiology

- Exercise Science

- Fitness and Health

- Fitness Science

- Golf Course Management

- Health Studies and Sports Management

- Health Therapies and Sports Fitness

- Leisure Management

- Leisure Studies

- Nutrition and Exercise Science

- Outdoor Activities

- Outdoor Studies

- Outdoor Studies and Sport

- Physical Activity, Exercise and Health

- Physical Education

- Physical Education and Sport

- Recreation Management

- Sport and Exercise Science

- Sport and Exercise Therapy

- Sport and Fitness Management

- Sport and Leisure

- Sport and Recreation

- Sport Conditioning, Rehabilitation and Coaching

- Sport, Health and Exercise

- Sport, Health and Fitness

- Sports and Leisure Management

- Sports Coaching and Development

- Sports Coaching with Sports Development

- Sports Development

- Sports Development and Physical Education

- Sports Leadership

- Sports Management

- Sports Nutrition

- Sports Psychology

- Sports Rehabilitation

- Sports Science

- Sports Science and Injury Management

- Sports Science and Physiology

- Sports Science – Water Sports and Adventure Activities Management

- Sports Studies

- Sports Technology

- Sports Therapy

- Turf Management.

PART-TIME STUDY

There will be plenty of opportunities to gain sport- and fitness-related qualifications while you are in employment. These range from the professional qualifications described on pages 72–6 to HNDs and foundation degrees.

HEALTH WARNING

When you are looking at different courses always check the content very carefully to make sure it is what you want! Courses with the same title don't necessarily cover exactly the same topics.

CHECKLIST

Here are some questions to ask when looking into courses:

- How is this course going to help my career?

- Is it recognised by employers and appropriate professional organisations?

- Can I afford to do it?

- Where do I get the money?

- Could I do the course by part-time study or distance learning?

SOURCES OF INFORMATION

- University and college prospectuses.

- University and college websites.

- Course leaflets.

- Alternative prospectuses (written by students and pretty realistic!).

- Higher education websites (see Chapter 4).

BEING PAID TO ENJOY YOUR SPORT

If you play a sport to a high standard (e.g. county level) and are thinking of applying to university it's worth finding out whether you might be eligible for a sports scholarship.

Quite a number of universities want to attract players of outstanding ability who will represent the university in national competitions. Students receive a bursary – which includes a non-repayable sum of money, professional coaching workshops, nutritional guidance and sports medicine services.

- Bath University gives sports scholarships of support costs up to £3,000 a year under the Talented Athlete Scholarship Scheme and free coaching and support facilities worth up to £2,000 to other selected students.

- Glasgow University awards sports bursaries consisting of financial assistance, access to sports science and medicine and physiotherapy back-up to high-level sportsmen and women.

- Kent County Cricket Club and the University of Kent provide cricket scholarships of £2,500 to students of high cricketing standard who are willing to play for Kent County Cricket Club.

- Northumbria University and Newcastle Rugby Football Union offer bursaries to assist students with training and other expenses.

In all cases, students study the subject of their choice. Many students go on to play sport professionally.

You can find information on sports scholarships in *University Scholarship, Awards and Bursaries*, published by Trotman.

THE TALENTED ATHLETE SCHOLARSHIP SCHEME (TASS)

TASS is a government-funded programme, managed by UK Sport, that distributes awards worth £3,000 per year to talented athletes who are committed to combining their sport and education. It aims to reduce the number of talented athletes dropping out of sport. Awards are made through individual universities and colleges. You can find out more about TASS at www.tass.gov.uk.

MATT STEVENS – POSTGRADUATE STUDENT, CARDIFF UNIVERSITY

Matt has completed a law degree at Cardiff and is now coming towards the end of a postgraduate legal practice course. All through his time at Cardiff he has held a Golf Bursary.

'I had captained the county Under-19 side and played in the Welsh squad before I came to university. Through a friend in the Welsh squad I heard about the bursary system. He told me that I would need a handicap of three or less and would have to be accepted on to a degree course. I could then apply. That is what I did. I chose Cardiff because it is not too far from home and I wanted to go back at weekends to play there.

'Golf scholarships are worth more than those for other sports because the money comes from the Royal and Ancient Golf Club. I get £1,500 to spend on equipment, travel expenses to tournaments and any extra coaching that I think I need. (I have to produce receipts to prove that the money has been spent on golf and not on general student expenses.) Golf is an expensive sport, so I am really pleased to have the bursary.

'The Royal and Ancient want to encourage young golf players who also have academic ambitions to stay in Britain, and if they eventually turn professional, play on the European Circuit rather than go to the USA. If they study there on sports scholarships, it is likely that they will stay in the USA.

'The university provides me with coaching, nutritional advice and help from a sports psychologist. All the sports scholars get dietary advice from the nutritionist, who works for the Welsh rugby team. She holds seminars and discussions for us at the university. We also have sessions with a sports psychology lecturer from UWIC (University of Wales College, Cardiff). He specialises in golf and is well-known on the

European Circuit. The seminars are really useful. I always leave them thinking, "I learned something today". Eight sessions are allowed each year. If I wanted more I could pay for them from my funding.

'My coach is Rob Butterworth, the Glamorgan and Wales coach. He is fantastic. In the winter there are not so many tournaments so I see him seven or eight times on a one-to-one basis to keep my game ticking over. We work at the driving range on minor points in my game. Rob videos me hitting balls, then plays the tape in slow motion and analyses my shots.

'As far as playing is concerned, I play in the league on Wednesdays and I do go back to play in my home team every Saturday. Other students do the same – and some travel greater distances. I have a friend who goes home to Surrey every Friday evening in order to play at his club there. During my degree course I managed to play three or four times a week but my timetable is heavier this year, so I put in more time at the range in the evenings.

'When I first came to university I had every intention of turning professional when I left. Things change, though – and I am now going to be a solicitor.'

So: there are lots of qualifications, different ways of getting them and different funding methods, *but* courses alone will not get you a job!

THE VALUE OF WORK EXPERIENCE

Advice from Heather Collier, Manager of the National Council for Work Experience:

'Work experience is becoming increasingly important for any student these days. With more students coming on to the job market every year, work experience helps you stand out from the crowd. Many employers expect to see a period of work experience on a CV and won't consider applications without any. A recent survey showed that it is one of the most successful ways of getting a permanent job. It is important though to start out by deciding just what you want and hope to achieve from a work experience placement, and to work out afterwards what you have gained from it. The time to bring this out is at a job interview when you can describe what you did and what you gained.'

Examples of work experience:

- holiday jobs on children's holiday play schemes

- part-time work as a leisure centre assistant

- part-time work as a lifeguard/pool attendant

- teaching an activity (if you have a relevant qualification) at a residential summer camp.

Why not qualify as soon as you can in one leisure activity – aerobics, say – and apply for work at a health club or leisure centre?

You get paid for all these jobs, too.

THE VALUE OF VOLUNTARY WORK

'I cannot stress enough the value of voluntary experience,' says Kevin Harris, a sports development officer. 'I soon found that you don't leave university and just walk into a job! It hit me that I needed a lot more experience and that voluntary work was the way to get it.' To see how he did this and got the job he wanted as a result, read his story on pages 65–7.

Luckily, there are lots and lots of openings for volunteers:

- at events like youth games

- helping with after-school games and sport in primary schools (or secondary schools if you are now in higher education)

- in coaching

- on summer sports programmes.

PAYING FOR QUALIFICATIONS

HOW MUCH?
That depends on how old you are and on exactly what you want to do. If, for example, you are 16 years old and thinking about staying in full-time education for two more years, you shouldn't have to pay very much. Full-time students under 19 years old normally don't pay tuition fees. (If you want to do a further education course and are over 19 years old, you'll probably be charged a few hundred pounds, but colleges can waive fees for students in financial difficulty.) Do expect, though, to pay for some visits organised as part of the course. You should also enquire from schools and colleges whether you might be eligible for an Educational Maintenance Bursary.

HIGHER EDUCATION
If you are planning to become a full-time student in higher education – i.e. on a degree or higher diploma course – you might have to make a contribution towards your tuition fees. At present universities and colleges may charge up to £3,070 per year, and all but a very small number do charge the maximum. (The figure rises each year in line with inflation.)

But you can take out a loan to cover the fees and you will not have to re-pay it until you have left your course and are earning £15,000 a year: then you will have to pay back 9% of your earnings.

It is always worth checking out what additional assistance is available. In addition to the specific sports scholarships already mentioned, there is a non-repayable grant of up to £2,765 a year available to students from low-income families to help with their living costs. Such students are also entitled to a further £305 from their universities and colleges *if* these institutions charge the maximum fee. There are additional grants for students with disabilities or students with children.

Scotland has a different system from the rest of the UK. Scottish students who live in Scotland and attend Scottish universities and colleges pay no tuition fees. However they do pay a Graduate Endowment – currently just over £2,300 – when they start work.

Then there are student loans for maintenance. These are paid back on the same terms as the tuition fee loans. The maximum amount that students may borrow each year is £6,315 for students in London and £4,735 for students elsewhere. The amounts available to you vary according to your family income and whether you live at home with your parents (for students under 25 years old). Students who receive the maintenance grant are entitled to smaller student loans.

If you are likely to be a mature student, there are other sources of financial help available for people with dependants or who are receiving state benefits. See *How to Get Financial Help as a Student* (details on page 100) for full information.

PROFESSIONAL QUALIFICATIONS
You are on your own here, unfortunately!

You would have to pay for your own training (unless you're sponsored by an employer), but there are ways of spreading the cost. Most organisations provide courses that can be taken on a part-time basis, which means that you can take on a part-time job – or even full-time, if you can juggle your hours – while training.

With a Career Development Loan you could borrow between £300 and £8,000 with the government paying the interest while you are on a full-time course. And you could get grants to cover travel and childcare. You would have to pay the loan back at a fixed rate of interest when the course finished. Career Development Loans are available through Barclays, the Co-operative Bank and the Royal Bank of Scotland. See www.lifelonglearning.co.uk.

SUMMING UP

After all you have read – is a career in sport and fitness for you? Would you like:

- the lifestyle

- the environment

- the salary potential?

Remember that all three can vary considerably according to where you are employed and in which area of the country you live.

And don't forget that there are promotion prospects. This is not an industry where entry levels and promotion prospects are rigid. You can get on: *but* it will be up to you to prove yourself by:

- being good at your job

- showing that you are willing to learn

- getting qualified, whether by working for NVQs in your job or taking further courses.

If you really want to get to the top areas of management, it will help to take further academic qualifications.

But qualifications are not enough on their own. People who carve out successful careers also have skills. You saw in Chapter 2 which skills are required to do some of the jobs well. To progress in a career, which invariably means taking on further responsibilities and being in charge of other people and their work, you need in addition to have some general skills. These are also known as transferable skills because they do not relate to just one career but to many.

What are transferable skills? How do you rate yourself on the following?

- **Communication skills** – being able to relate well to people from a wide range of backgrounds, putting your ideas across effectively, explaining to colleagues or junior staff what you want them to do.

- **Commitment** – being dependable, punctual, giving a lot to your work.

- **Customer service** – keeping customers and clients happy, sorting out any complaints they have, listening to their suggestions.

- **Leadership** – taking responsibility and managing other people, getting things done.

- **Problem-solving skills** – getting around difficulties, finding a way round problems.

- **Resourcefulness** – using your initiative, planning ahead, adapting and changing your plans if you have to.

- **Teamwork skills** – working well with other people and being able to give and take.

These are the top skills that employers come up with time and time again when asked which transferable skills they rate most highly.

A job in sport and fitness does not have to be your first. There is plenty of room for career changers. If you are feel you are getting nowhere, feel trapped or bored to tears in your present job – go for it. Ask yourself a few questions first, though:

Am I too old?
Age isn't too important, but your level of fitness (if you want an active job) is.

Can I afford a drop in salary?
Anyone moving to a new career – in whatever area – is more than likely going to have to take a cut in salary while re-training and gaining experience. Career changers need to be realistic about family commitments.

If you're thinking about a full-time course:

I haven't done any study for a long time. Will my brain cope?
Yes. More and more mature students enrol on courses every year. Interestingly, many more mature students are training in physiotherapy than used to be the case.

Will I get a job at the end of the course?
No one can predict or guarantee this, but course tutors should have a good idea of where past students are working. So should the college or university careers service. Ask!

CHAPTER 4

Next steps

WHERE TO GET ADVICE

If you are still at school, you should find lots of information in your careers room or library. This should contain many of the books and information from the sources that are recommended in the next chapter. You should also be able to access the internet in school and look at information on the various websites (also recommended in the next chapter). And of course, if you have internet access at home you can research there. If you want advice, talk to your careers teacher and the careers adviser who visits your school. In Northern Ireland, Scotland and Wales, careers advisers work for local careers services. In England they may be known as personal advisers (careers) and may work for the Connexions Service. Careers advisers should be able to point you in the right direction for advice and information. They will also be able to help you decide on your most suitable route and entry point for your career in sports and fitness.

If you are in higher education, make contact with your careers advisory service. You will find information on different careers in their information rooms; you will be able to use computer programs that link your skills and interests to particular jobs and you will be able to use the graduate careers advisory service system (www.prospects.ac.uk) – which contains a wealth of information on careers, training, courses and salaries. You should also be able to book an appointment for an individual guidance session with a careers adviser.

Many higher education careers services also offer:

- information sessions on career areas (e.g. the leisure industry)

- job fairs which are visited by employers

- the opportunity to get some relevant work experience

- seminars and workshops on job hunting, CV writing, applications and interviews.

These things really do matter. Graduates – the most highly educated members of the population – often find their applications rejected for the following reasons:

- They send their CVs and letters to the wrong person. (It only takes a few minutes to ring the employer and ask where they should be sent!)

- They send letters and CVs that include grammar and spelling mistakes. (Never rely on your computer's spell check system. It can come up with some odd ideas. Use an old-fashioned dictionary.)

- They turn up to interviews knowing very little about the company. (What's so difficult about logging on to their websites?)

Entire books have been written on applying for jobs and on interview techniques. You can also find advice on the Prospects website.

If you are a graduate, you may continue to use the services of your careers advisory service (although some have a cut-off point of a certain number of years after graduation) – and if you no longer live near your old campus, you can try contacting the careers service at your nearest higher education careers service. Many offer help to graduates from other universities and colleges. Another method is to pay for careers guidance in the private sector. A consultation with such an organisation will probably include psychometric tests followed by discussion and recommendations. Costs and standards of service vary widely – and can cost several thousand pounds. You can find organisations advertising on the internet if you key 'careers advice' into one of the search engines. You can also complete some tests and interest questionnaires on the internet. Why not try these first and see what you think of the results?

The main thing to remember is that there is a lot of information out there and several sources of advice. Make sure that you get as much help as possible.

HOW TO FIND A JOB IN SPORT AND FITNESS

The press is a good starting point. National newspapers advertise public sector jobs on different days of the week. Wednesday's *Guardian* is good for jobs in leisure, including recreation management and sports development. Jobs in education are advertised in the *Guardian* on Tuesdays, the *Independent* on Thursdays and *The Times Educational Supplement* and *The Times Higher Education Supplement* on Fridays. Posts for coaches and sports development officers are advertised here as well as teaching jobs. If you are looking for a job in the area where you currently live, try your local newspaper. This should be a good source of junior positions such as leisure centre/sports centre assistant, as well as management jobs.

Professional magazines are another good source. You should be able to find copies in a reference library. Try *Leisure Management* and *Hospitality* (includes some jobs in leisure).

Noticeboards are worth investigating. Put on your walking shoes, go to the nearest gym, health club, leisure centre and see if any vacancies are advertised.

Many, many jobs are now advertised on the internet. There are lots of websites for job hunters. Try putting the words 'sport' and 'jobs' into any of the major search engines – and away you go. Particularly useful is www.leisureopportunities.co.uk, which advertises a range of jobs, including the following: tennis managers, club managers and assistant managers, fitness instructors, duty officers (leisure centres), young people's sports and activities co-ordinators, spa managers, gym instructors, reception managers, specialist physical activity officers (mental health), outdoor sport and leisure managers.

Try the websites of any of the professional associations listed in Chapter 5; and www.jobsgopublic.com, which advertises jobs in sport and leisure on behalf of local authorities.

Don't forget careers services. They may receive job details direct from employers. They will also know of employers you could approach with a speculative application.

APPRENTICESHIPS

Ask your careers adviser. You can also find information on the internet at:

- www.apprenticeships.org.uk (England)

- www.modernapprenticeships.com (Scotland)

- www.elwa.org.uk (Wales).

CHAPTER 5

Further information

PUBLICATIONS

Careers 2008, Trotman – a general careers guide with useful,
relevant chapters

A Guide to Qualifications in Sport and Recreation, Institute of
Leisure and Amenities Management, ILAM (to be revised by
ISPAL)

How to Get Financial Help as a Student, Department for Education
and Skills, free by calling 0800 587 8500 (www.direct.gov.uk/
en/educationandlearning); or from Student Support Branch,
Department for Employment and Learning, Northern Ireland,
tel: 028 9025 7710 (www.studentfinanceni.co.uk); or the
Students Awards Agency for Scotland, tel: 0131 476 8212
(www.saas.gov.uk)

Institute of Sport and Recreation Management Information Pack,
Institute of Sport and Recreation Management

Leisure Management, AGCAS

The Penguin Careers Guide – a general careers guide and
reference book

HIGHER EDUCATION
Directory of University and College Entry 2008/9, Trotman
Entrance Guide to Higher Education in Scotland, UCAS/
Universities Scotland

UCAS Directory – for a list of higher education courses
University and College Entrance: The Official Guide, UCAS
University Scholarships, Awards and Bursaries, Trotman

USEFUL ORGANISATIONS

British Association of Sport and Exercise Sciences
114 Cardigan Road
Headingley LS6 3BJ
Tel: 0113 289 1020
www.bases.org.uk

British Olympic Association
1 Wandsworth Plain
London SW18 1EH
Tel: 020 8871 2677
www.olympics.org.uk

British Paralympic Association
BPA, Norwich Union Building
9th Floor, 69 Park Lane
Croydon CR9 1BG
Tel: 020 7662 888
www.paralympics.org.uk

England and Wales Cricket Board
Lords Cricket Ground
London NW8 8QZ
Tel: 020 7432 1200
www.ecb.co.uk

The Football Association
25 Soho Square
London W1D 4FA
Tel: 020 7745 4545
www.the-fa.org

Footballers' Further Education and Vocational Training Society Ltd
2 Oxford Court
Manchester M2 3WQ
Tel: 0161 236 0637

Institute for Outdoor Learning
The Barn, Plumpton Old Hall
Plumpton
Penrith CA11 9NP
Tel: 01768 885800
www.outdoor-learning.org

Institute for Sports, Parks and Leisure
The Grotto House
Lower Basildon
Reading RG8 9NE
Tel: 0845 603 8734
www.ispal.co.uk

Institute of Groundsmanship
19–23 Church Street
Wolverton MK12 5LG
Tel: 01908 312511
www.iog.org.uk

Institute of Sport and Recreational Management
Sir John Beckwith Centre for Sport
Loughborough University
Loughborough LE11 3TU
Tel: 01509 226474
www.isrm.co.uk

The Lawn Tennis Association
100 Priory Lane
London SW15 5JQ
Tel: 020 8487 7000
www.lta.org.uk

Lifesavers (Royal Life Saving Society)
River House
High Street
Broom B50 4HN
Tel: 01789 773 994
www.lifesavers.org.uk

Mountain Leader Training Board
177 Burton Road
West Didsbury M20 2BB
Tel: 0161 445 4747
www.mltb.org

National Register of Personal Trainers
PO Box 3455
Marlow SL7 1WG
Tel: 0870 20060
www.nrpt.co.uk

Premier Training International
Premier House
Willowside Park
Canal Road
Trowbridge BA14 8RH
Tel: 01225 353535
www.premierglobal.co.uk

The Professional Golfers' Association
Centenary House
The Belfry
Sutton Coldfield B76 9PT
Tel: 01675 470333
www.pga.org.uk

Professional Players Federation
3rd Floor
10 Bow Lane
London EC4M 9AL
Tel: 020 7236 5148
http://ppf.org.uk

Register of Exercise Professionals
8–10 Crown Hill
Croydon CR0 1RZ
Tel: 020 8686 6464
www.exerciseregister.org

SkillsActive (Sector Skills Council for Active Leisure and Learning)
Castlewood House
77–91 New Oxford Street
London WC1A 1PX
Tel: 020 7632 2000
www.skillsactive.com

SkillsActive Northern Ireland
68 Dunmore Road
Ballynahinch BT24 8PR
Tel: 0289 756 0002

SkillsActive Scotland
28 Castle Street
Edinburgh EH2 3HT
Tel: 0131 226 6618
www.skillsactive.com

SkillsActive Wales
c/o Sports Council for Wales (address below)

The Society of Sports Therapists
16 Royal Terrace
Glasgow G3 7NY
Tel: 0845 600 2613
www.society-of-sports-therapists.org

Sport England
3rd Floor, Victoria House
London WC1B 4SE
Tel: 08458 508508
www.sportengland.org

Sport Scotland
Caledonia House
1 Redheughs Rigg
South Gyle EH12 9DQ
Tel: 0131 317 7200
www.sportscotland.org.uk

Sports Coach UK (National Coaching Federation)
114 Cardigan Road
Headingley LS6 3BJ
Tel: 0113 274 4802
www.sportscoachuk.org

The Sports Council for Northern Ireland
House of Sport
Upper Malone Road
Belfast BT9 5LA
Tel: 028 9038 1222
www.sportni.net

Sports Council for Wales/Cyngor Chwaraeon Cymru
Welsh Institute of Sport/Athrofa Chwaraeon Cymru
Sophia Gardens/Gerddi Sophia
Cardiff/Caerdydd CF11 9SW
Tel: 029 2064 4526
www.sports-council-wales.org.uk

The Swimming Teachers' Association
Anchor House
Birch Street
Walsall WS2 8HZ
Tel: 01922 645097
www.sta.co.uk

UK Sport (The UK Sports Council)
40 Bernard Street
London WC1N 1ST
Tel: 020 7211 5100
www.uksport.gov.uk

Universities and Colleges Admissions Service (UCAS)
Rosehill
New Barn Lane
Cheltenham GL52 3LZ
Tel: 01242 227788
www.ucas.com

YMCA Fitness Industry Training
111 Great Russell Street
London WC1B 3NP
Tel: 020 7343 1850
www.ymcafit.org.uk

Yoga Biomedical Trust
90–92 Pentonville Road
London N1 9HS
Tel: 020 7689 3040
www.yogatherapy.org

OTHER WEBSITES

www.direct.gov.uk/en/educationandlearning (England)
www.studentfinanceni.co.uk (Northern Ireland)
www.saas.gov.uk (Scotland)
www.studentfinancewales.co.uk (Wales)
www.tass.gov.uk (sports scholarships)
www.jobsgopublic.com
www.monster.co.uk
www.prospects.ac.uk (a careers site for students in higher education)